THE
SHAKESPEARE TERCENTENARY
OF 1864

The Shakespeare Tercentenary of 1864

RICHARD FOULKES
with a Foreword by J C Trewin

THE SOCIETY FOR THEATRE RESEARCH

First published 1984
by The Society for Theatre Research
77 Kinnerton Street, London SW1X 8ED

ISBN 0 85430 038 4

Printed in Great Britain at
The Pitman Press, Bath

Contents

Illustrations

STRATFORD

between pages 24 and 25

E F Flower (from *The Illustrated London News* 7 May 1864)
The Rev. J C M Bellew (courtesy of the National Portrait Gallery, London)
The Stratford Tercentenary ribbon (from the author's collection)
The exterior of the Pavilion (from *The Illustrated Times* 30 April 1864)
The Banquet at the Pavilion (from *The Illustrated Times* 30 April 1864)
The Messiah at the Pavilion (from *The Illustrated London News* 7 May 1864)
The Fancy Dress Ball at the Pavilion (from *The Illustrated London News* 14 May 1864)
Twelfth Night at the Pavilion (from *The Illustrated London News* 7 May 1864)

LONDON

between pages 48 and 49

J O Halliwell (from the Record Office, Stratford-upon-Avon)
Proposed Design for the National Shakespeare Memorial (cartoon from *The Illustrated Times* 6 February 1864)
Celebrations at the Crystal Palace (from *The Illustrated London News* 30 April 1864)
Concert at the Agricultural Hall (from *The Illustrated London News* 30 April 1864)
Romeo and Juliet at the Princess's (from *The Illustrated London News* 7 May 1864)
Henry IV i at Drury Lane (from *The Illustrated Times* 9 April 1864)
The Battle of Shrewsbury at Drury Lane (from *The Illustrated London News* 30 April 1864)
The planting of the Shakespeare Oak on Primrose Hill (from *The Illustrated Times* 30 April 1864)

Grateful acknowledgement is made to the Central Photographic Unit, University of Leicester, for taking the photographs for illustrations, and to the University of Leicester Library for providing the original journals.

Foreword

When I first went to Stratford-upon-Avon long ago, a noticeable group of tall poplars stood behind the houses of Old Town. It marked the place where the Grand Pavilion had been in 1864 for the local celebration of the Tercentenary of Shakespeare's birth.

Stratford was still a small market-town, though the railway had just reached it, and the Mayor, Edward Fordham Flower, could speak of "these railway times". It was fifteen years before the first Memorial Theatre was built by the river. Too often a theatre history of Stratford begins with the Memorial (after a glance at what happened to Garrick on those drenching days and nights in 1769). General stage histories are inclined to gloss over the Tercentenary in either London or Warwickshire. Now Richard Foulkes has done what has been needed, and described, lucidly and wittily, with the benefit of sustained research and informed hindsight, what did go on, and why, in that resolute straining towards the Birthday (and after). Stratford's contribution to the events of 1864 was something of which Robert Hunter, writing at the time, could leave only a record choked with detail.

The story, of course, is London's as much as Stratford's. A complicated business, it proved, among a good deal else, the danger of celebration by committee, the National Shakespeare Committee, the Stratford Committee, the Working Men's Shakespeare Committee, and so on, all manfully determined to do something. The Stratford men showed themselves, as Mr Foulkes admirably describes, to be entirely tactless. They had no idea of the particular sensibilities of such an actor as Samuel Phelps or such an actress as Helen Faucit, or why A could not be invited if B was, or what exactly must be done at a given time. As told here, the whole tale, local and metropolitan, with its side-issues, fascinatingly unravels a tangled skein: a clear look at a matter where Stratford and London had never seemed so far apart. Still, the Earl of Warwick had no doubt that it would be a splendid affair. Had not the town shown "at the Agricultural Show, some years ago, what it could do on such occasions"?

J.C.T.

Acknowledgements

Whilst the Garrick Shakespeare Jubilee has been the subject of two full length books no comparable account had been made, hitherto, of the Shakespeare Tercentenary. That is not to say that it has been completely neglected, indeed it has been fortunate in receiving the attention of such distinguished scholars as J C Trewin, whose *The Night Has Been Unruly* incorporated a chapter on the Tercentenary, and T J B Spencer and Stanley Wells who contributed one to *Shakespeare: A Celebration*. I am indebted to them all and add a further debt of gratitude to John Trewin, whom the Society for Theatre Research invited to edit this volume thereby making me the beneficiary of his incomparable knowledge and unflagging enthusiasm.

From the narrow focus of an April day in 1864 my research spread outwards in many absorbing directions leading me to libraries and collections far and wide in which was reposited some Tercentenary nugget. Sources are acknowledged in the text, but I am especially beholden to Mrs. Marian Pringle and her colleagues at the Shakespeare Birthplace Trust Library, the Shakespeare Centre, Stratford-upon-Avon and to Dr. Robert Bearman at the Record Office, Stratford-upon-Avon. Towards the end of my research I was privileged to receive a British Academy award which, together with a grant from the University of Leicester Research Board, enabled me to visit the Folger Shakespeare Library in Washington, DC, and the Harvard Theatre Collection. The Folger Library was a fitting place in which to conclude my research since it was Ralph Waldo Emerson's comments on the Shakespeare Tercentenary that inspired Henry Clay Folger to embark upon his unique collection.[1]

Of the many correspondents who have answered my enquiries I must single out Professor Philip Collins and Lady Flower. To Miss Pat Perkins I express my appreciation for her unerring skill in translating my labrynthine manuscript into a pristine typescript. My particular gratitude is due to Dr. Kathleen Barker and Emeritus Professor H A Jones, CBE, both of whom found time to read my first, considerably longer, draft and gave me the benefit of their reactions to it. Finally I am obliged to my family upon whom the encroachments of the Shakespeare Tercentenary must have rivalled those experienced by their Victorian counterparts.

Richard Foulkes
University Centre, Northampton

1. The Prospectus of The Folger Shakespeare Library reads: "After hearing Emerson and reading his essay on the tercentenary of Shakespeare's birth. . . . Folger soon purchased an inexpensive set of Shakespeare's works – the beginning of what has become the largest collection in the world of Shakespeare's printed works". Emerson's essay did not appear in print until 1904 (*Atlantic Monthly* v. 94, September 1904 pp. 365–7) so Folger may have known it in an earlier form. Emerson corresponded with and visited the Flowers in Stratford.

The Beginnings

It was the great eighteenth-century actor David Garrick who first embarked upon the serious business of celebrating Shakespeare at Stratford with the Jubilee to celebrate the bi-centenary of Shakespeare's birth held, belatedly, in September 1769. The history of Garrick's Jubilee has been extensively chronicled[1] and its relevance to the Tercentenary in 1864 lies in the extent to which the later event was influenced by the earlier. The principal importance of Garrick's Jubilee was that the foremost actor of the day was prepared to come to Shakespeare's birthplace, then an unexceptional Midland market-town, to celebrate him there rather than in London, thereby establishing a vital precedent.

Garrick's motives were not entirely altruistic, he saw the Jubilee as an opportunity, unfulfilled as it turned out, to enhance his own reputation, and with this in mind the programme was directed principally towards well-to-do visitors, mainly from London, and the local gentry, rather than the citizens of Stratford. Such events as the public breakfast, Handel's *Judith*, the "Ordinary" (songs, ballads and glees) and the grand fancy-dress ball were aimed at more discerning and better-off patrons and the one event designed to appeal to the locals – the Pageant – was abandoned because of the weather, although Garrick's delivery of his Ode to Shakespeare, with which the procession was to have ended, still took place, indoors. Thus began the long-standing tension between performers, visitors and locals. The locals resented their exclusion from most of the celebrations and their subservient servicing role; visitors became convinced – justifiably or not – of the rapacity of the town's tradesmen.

Stratford possessed no building capable of accommodating Garrick's diverse and ambitious programme, and so he had constructed on the banks of the Avon a building known as the Rotunda (said to be based on that at Ranelagh). As the torrential rain fell and the river rose, the Rotunda's shortcomings became manifest, but at least it was purpose-built, the forerunner of more commodious and better placed constructions.

Garrick realised that the Jubilee would be a costly venture. He failed in his attempt to get the Town Council to underwrite it and, although certain Stratfordians contributed up to £100 each, Garrick lost some £2,000,[2] though this was mitigated by the success of the restaged pageant at Drury Lane later in the year. Thus arose the recurring problem of how Stratford should meet the cost of honouring its most famous son and the debate as to whether the town was the net gainer or loser financially.

One historian has dubbed the 1769 Jubilee "Garrick's Folly" and certainly the actor allowed his normally canny judgement to be clouded by his desire for personal aggrandisement. However, not all difficulties were of his making and Stratford was fortunate in this pioneering venture to have the services of the undisputed leader of the theatrical profession. When the Secretary of the Stratford Tercentenary, Robert Hunter, wrote his record of that event, he observed wistfully:

> Happy would it have been for the Stratford Committee during the late celebration, if an actor so accomplished and generous had been forthcoming and permitted to take full charge of the dramatic portion of the business. They would have been spared vast labour, no end of anxiety and enormous pecuniary expenditure.[3]

Garrick hoped that Jubilees would become regular events, but it took another London actor to revive local interest. In 1814 Charles Mathews made his first appearance in Stratford and was appalled by the "miserable barn" with its capacity of £28 in which he performed. When he returned in December 1820 he instigated a meeting at the Town Hall "to consider the best mode of erecting, in the form of a theatre, a national monument to the immortal memory of Shakespeare".[4] The vicar and mayor lent strong support and Mathews was elected president and treasurer with a view to enlisting support from "every poet, artist and sculptor whom he was fortunate enough to know"[5] as well as the King himself. Alas, Mathews' imaginative enthusiasm was not matched by the metropolitan response. The theatre scheme was diluted into one for a statue, which Nash was to design, but a typical response was that of Lord Egremont:

> I consider the fame and genius of Shakespeare to be the property of the whole kingdom, and I cannot consent to confine it to the town of Stratford. . . . I therefore hope that the statue may be placed in the metropolis.[6]

This metropolitan disdain dogged Stratford for the rest of the century, but it may have put the town on its mettle, for in 1824 the Shakespeare Club was formed and three years later it organised a Jubilee. The town's predilection for a pageant asserted itself, and the Mayor proceeded from Holy Trinity to New Place, accompanied by fifty constables, a military band, and Francis Raymond's theatrical company from Northampton dressed as Shakespearean characters.[7] In the garden of New Place the Mayor formally laid the corner stone of Stratford's first theatre, which was already under construction. This theatre survived until 1872, but by the middle of the century its principal use was as a court-room, and it had become an obstacle to the excavation and restoration of New Place Gardens.

Another festival took place in 1830 when the completed theatre was used for performances and a Pavilion was erected in Rother Street, but the highlight was again a pageant, in which the youthful Charles Kean took a prominent part. In both 1827 and 1830 the town, principally by virtue of the Pageant, attracted hordes of visitors from the local county and conurbations, which meant good business for the tradesmen of Stratford, who were the moving force behind the arrangements, but to the local gentry and the casual observer from London it all seemed "a Brummagem affair".

By the 1840s Stratford was attracting more discerning visitors. The Birthplace was purchased by subscription in 1847 with the help of actors (Macready), writers (Dickens) and politicians, including the Sixth Earl of Carlisle, who was then Chief Commissioner for Woods and Forests in Lord John Russell's Liberal administration. During the 1840s J O Halliwell (later Halliwell-Phillips) embarked on his extensive Shakespearean studies. He acquired an important collection of Shakespearean books at George Chalmers's sale in 1840; in 1848 he published his *Life of William Shakespeare*; in 1853 the first of his Folio editions appeared; in 1862 he arranged the bulk of the Stratford records, meeting the cost of the catalogue himself; and in 1864 his *History of New Place* was published.

Halliwell's interest in Shakespeareana was not confined to scholarly publications. In 1861 he led the National Shakespeare Fund in the acquisition of New Place and in an appeal to purchase the gardens before October 25, when "in all probability the gardens of Shakespeare will be handed over to the speculator";[8] he proceeded with the purchase at a cost of £3,400 when the appeal had reached only £2,401. Halliwell occupied a pivotal position in the Stratford-London Shakespearean axis; he was London-based and promoted his fund-raising here, but he knew Stratford and was respected there. By temperament he was unassertive and observed the rivalry between Stratford and London fully aware of its destructiveness, but incapable of imposing the harmony which he hoped for and which he alone might have commanded; instead he wrote plaintively, "For myself I am absolutely passive".[9] Of other leading Shakespearean scholars John Payne Collier was by then infirm and discredited by the so-called Perkins Folio forgeries and took no part in the celebrations.

The credit for alerting Stratford to the approaching Tercentenary of Shakespeare's birth belonged to Harries Tilbury, a celebrated comedian, who, at the Shakespeare Club dinner on April 23 1859, proclaimed: "'Time with his stealing steps' will quickly bear to you the year 1864".[10] During 1860 the Revd. G Granville, Vicar of Stratford, sought the support of sympathetic noblemen, in particular Lord Leigh of Stoneleigh Abbey, Lord Lieutenant of the County, and the Earl of Carlisle. Lord Leigh, whilst he had not inherited the literary disposition of his father Chandos Leigh, was equally diligent in all he undertook. The Earl of Carlisle had been sympathetic at the time of the acquisition of the Birthplace and his distinction as a scholar and poet as well as a politician (Lord Lieutenant of Ireland 1855–58 and 1859–64) made his Presidency as appropriate as it was prestigious. Another nobleman who was to serve Stratford well was Sir Robert Collie North Hamilton who, having played a vital part in the restoration of order in Central India after the 1857 mutiny, retired because of ill-health to Avon Cliffe near Stratford and took a lively interest in local affairs, though his attempt to get elected as the Liberal MP for South Warwickshire in 1868 was unsuccessful.

However a measure of the mental barrier amongst some of the local gentry is revealed in a letter from the Earl of Warwick:

> I have no doubt it will be a splendid affair, for the town of Stratford proved at the Agricultural Show, some years ago, what it could do on such occasions.[11]

The support of the local nobility was vital and such preconceptions had to be overcome if the celebrations were to be a success in social or financial terms. The contributions of the aristocracy and gentry to the funds were essential; admission prices were geared to them; and without them Stratford's efforts could not hope to be more than local. On the other hand such patronage inevitably provoked the feeling in Stratford that the Tercentenary was just for the "nobs".

It took some time for Granville's soundings to be consolidated into any formal structure. A Tercentenary Committee was formed at the Town Hall on 22 July 1861; at the birthday dinner in 1862 a local tragedian, James Bennett, alerted members to the task ahead; and by the spring of 1863 a draft programme had been prepared. Although Stratfordians realised the need for outside patronage if their Tercentenary were to succeed, it was equally essential to have committed and hard-working local supporters. Granville was a cultivated man with artistic connections such as the Rev. J C M Bellew, Charles Fechter and Edmund Yates who "were most hospitably entertained"[12] by him in June 1862. James Bennett had many professional contacts, though his self-interest sometimes overshadowed that of the Tercentenary. A local medical practitioner, Dr. Kingsley, acted as Honorary Secretary, and many tradesmen such as James Cox, the builder, offered expert advice. But for Stratford to succeed, it needed the complete commitment of a man who could command respect nationally. Fortunately such a man was at hand in the person of Edward Flower.

Edward Fordham Flower was born in 1805, the youngest son of Richard Flower, a brewer and landowner of Marden Hall, Hertfordshire. Although the Flowers were prosperous entrepreneurs they were by no means conventional, being Unitarian in religion and radical in politics. Richard's elder brother Benjamin, a notable political writer and dissenter, was hostile to the war with France, and together with Richard founded a monthly magazine, *The Political Register*, which flourished between 1807 and 1811. Benjamin had two talented daughters: Eliza, a composer, and Sarah (Flower Adams), a poetess, who had close links with like-minded families such as the Martineaus and that of W J Fox, as well as literary acquaintances in Dickens and Browning.

Richard Flower became disenchanted with the heavy taxation and political illiberalism of Britain and considered emigration to France, but his eldest son George was persuaded by General Lafayette to try

America. Early in 1816 George Flower and his friend Morris Birkbeck went on an exploratory visit as a result of which the Flowers bought 20,000 acres of land at what was to become the city of Albion.[13] Richard Flower sold up his English property for £23,000 and hired two ships from Liverpool to take his family and retinue of over 100 to the New World.

There Edward's upbringing lacked much formal education, but he made up for this by developing his natural gifts of resourcefulness, energy and determination. In 1824 Richard Flower returned to England with his youngest son and they visited Robert Owen's New Lanark community, an early and then successful socialist experiment. Here Flower negotiated Owen's purchase of the New Harmony settlement where Owen hoped to repeat his Scottish experiment.

Although his father returned to America, Edward settled in Britain, spending six months in New Lanark before marrying Selina Greaves of Barford. Richard gave his son £2,000 with which Edward built a house by the Avon in Stratford and set up as a timber merchant, specialising in cooperage. On Richard's death in 1830 Edward succeeded to the remaining English family property, disposed of his timber business to James Cox and built a brewery, the first in Stratford.

Three sons were born in three years and in due course the eldest (Charles) and youngest (Edgar) joined the firm, whilst the middle son (later Sir) William had a distinguished career in medicine. The family flair for business brought rapid results, by 1857 annual sales apparently amounted to £41,566 of which about £20,000 was profit; and by 1866 sales were approaching £100,000 a year.[14] This prosperity enabled Edward to enjoy a grand life-style, in 1855 the family moved into The Hill, a large house on the Warwick Road; he was Mayor of Stratford in 1851 and 1852 and later an unsuccessful Liberal candidate for Coventry (1865) and North Warwickshire (1868).

It was no surprise, therefore, that "in anticipation of the 'Tercentenary', a numerously-signed requisition from the inhabitants was sent to induce him to become Mayor, that he might take a leading part in celebrating this occasion".[15] Charles's wife Sarah, née Martineau, kept a diary in which the first reference to the Tercentenary appears in June 1863:

> Beginning to talk about the Shakespeare Tercentenary. Mr. Flower being Mayor, and expecting to be so for the great year (1864) and has set his mind upon carrying out all that has to be done with spirit, but everyone has some particular notion of his own about keeping April 23rd next and it was hard to come to any agreement.[16]

Disagreement centred on two aspects of the Tercentenary: fund-raising and the purpose for which such money should be used; and the content of the festival programme. The difficulties affecting the festival programme arose more from the negotiations with artistes than any fundamental disagreement within the Stratford Committee; it was in the matter of fund-raising that the deepest divisions lay.

Such was the spirit of utilitarianism abroad in mid-Victorian England that no-one involved in Tercentenary celebrations considered that they might be an end in themselves, an opportunity for people to enjoy the moment for what it was worth. Instead it was generally accepted that the Tercentenary should be directed to some tangible and worthy end.

As early as 1859 Harries Tilbury, in his speech at the Shakespeare Club dinner had suggested that funds should be raised to endow scholarships at a University for pupils from the town's Grammar School. In 1861 the proposal was to purchase the New Place Garden, the remainder of the Birthplace Estate, Anne Hathaway's cottage, Getby's copyhold and any other properties connected with Shakespeare. This list shows a strong affinity with the objectives of Halliwell's National Shakespeare Fund which was getting underway in the same year. At a County Meeting at the Town Hall on May 28 1863, with Lord Leigh in the chair, James Bennett argued that the celebrations should aim at attracting national support "And that a memorial statue be erected on an appropriate spot in Shakespeare's town of Stratford-upon-Avon".[17] He was supported by James Cox, the local builder, but Flower himself replied that although "he could not himself give preference to a statue before the school, as Mayor of the town, he should be happy to assist in carrying out any scheme that might be decided upon".[18] The vote was 32–32; Lord Leigh cast the chair's vote against the statue proposal.

The monument party would not let matters rest and called another meeting, doubtfully constitutional, at which Cox proposed that "no scheme for the commemoration of the three hundredth anniversary of our great national poet can be considered complete that does not embrace as a prominent feature a statue or monumental memorial in this his native town".[19] This proposal was carried overwhelmingly and in spite of their personal reservations Lord Leigh and Flower felt obliged to accept it, though as a compromise donors could specify how their contribution was to be allocated – Lord Leigh stipulated that his donation of 100 gns. (£105) should go exclusively to the scholarship fund, though it was later transferred to the festival fund.

Stratford was now committed to an objective which was to prove to be a major embarrassment. Possessing, as the town did, many Shakespearean relics in an imperfect state of repair or still in private ownership, it seemed perverse to many that priority should be given to the erection of a statue or monument. Even the quiescent Halliwell experienced exasperation as he found Stratford eschewing the causes for which he had worked so hard. But there were further complications, for Stratford was not alone in its Tercentenary planning and its predilection for a monument was taken as a calculated challenge by certain parties who were concerning themselves with metropolitan celebrations.

Halliwell's National Shakespeare Fund was the obvious focus for metropolitan activity. Since its inception in 1861 it had gathered around it many distinguished supporters under the Presidency of the Duke of Newcastle. On 26 June 1863 Charles and Ellen Kean gave a programme of

"Readings and Recitations at St..James's Hall . . . for the benefit of the National Shakespeare Fund . . . their last public appearance in London prior to their departure for Australia".[20] "The hall was completely filled at an early hour by an exceedingly appreciative and fashionable audience".[21] Charles Kean's social standing was unique in the theatre of the time; his disreputable father had sent him to Eton and thereafter Charles cultivated aristocratic connections: "In Dublin he became a frequent guest at the Castle and the Park under . . . the Chief Secretaryship of the Earl of Carlisle (then Lord Morpeth)".[22] He had been Master of the Queen's Theatricals at Windsor and his election as a F.S.A. in 1857 was the greatest honour hitherto bestowed upon an actor and a recognition of the painstaking historical accuracy of his productions at the Princess's Theatre in the 1850s.

The Keans' absence in Australia during the Tercentenary celebrations invites speculation about the course of events had they been in England – might they have provided the unifying element or would they have added to the professional rivalries which beset the event? One goal which Kean might well have been able to achieve for the Tercentenary was the Royal Patronage which eluded both the London and Stratford committees.

It was not in Halliwell's nature to exclude anyone from his cause: the Earl of Carlisle, Sir Robert Hamilton and Flower himself were members of his committee and he wrote sympathetically to Dr. Kingsley in Stratford:

> Pray do not talk about interrupting me; at any and all times I shall be not only much pleased but flattered at being asked any questions you think it may be in my power to answer . . . at least 3 committees are already forming in London!! I do not see how in any case your scheme can be interfered with. It will be awful work if there is no end of the separate committees all working separately.[23]

The two London committees, apart from the Shakespeare Fund, were the Urban Club and the Royal Dramatic College. The Urban Club, originally "The Friday Knights", was founded in 1856 by certain members of "The Re-Union" club who lived in North London. It met at the Old Jerusalem Tavern in St. John's Gate Clerkenwell and the highlights of its year were the Foundation Supper in November and the Shakespeare Commemoration on 23 April. Members included Clement Scott, Westland Marston, John Oxenford, Henry Morley, Dr. Doran, Hepworth Dixon, Edmund Yates and Cordy Jeaffreson.[24] Its fund-raising objective for the Tercentenary was the erection of a monument.

The Royal Dramatic College was the brainchild of a group of prominent actors, all members of the Garrick Club. It was launched in July 1858 at a meeting presided over by Charles Kean, who defined its purpose as: "To provide an asylum for some of those who, having long administered to your amusement, seek rest and comfort for the evening of their lives".[25] The College acquired Royal Patronage and its trustees included Charles Kean, Dickens and Thackeray, but the driving force was Ben Webster who was designated the Master. After wranglings over a site in Buckinghamshire, the Royal Dramatic College was located in Woking on land acquired from the London Necropolis Company, which gave rise to some fairly obvious jokes. The foundation stone of the College was laid on 1 June 1860 by the Prince Consort, who expressed the view that "the importance cannot be over-rated of endeavouring to combine with . . . amusement . . . instruction and self-improvement".[26]

Unfortunately though the Royal Dramatic College was an attempt to rescue the acting profession from its reputation for financial improvidence, it served only to re-enforce it. By 1863 some £28,000 had been raised and all but spent, leaving little to support the handful of elderly pensioners in residence. The Tercentenary seemed an ideal opportunity to bolster the College's flagging fortunes and to launch its expansion into a school for actors' children, who would receive a good general education, opening up wider career prospects than those enjoyed by their parents. Such an objective accorded closely with the University scholarships for local pupils proposed in Stratford.

Three committees with three different objectives: the Shakespeare Fund – the Stratford properties; the Urban Club – a monument; the Royal Dramatic College – its own endowment. Who could unite such diverse ambitions? Certainly not Halliwell, but there was one man who seemed to be waiting for just such an occasion – W Hepworth Dixon. Dixon, as a Deputy Commissioner, had been responsible for starting one hundred of the three hundred committees constituted for the Great Exhibition, which itself seemed to be his exemplar for the Tercentenary. By then the museums paid for by the Exhibition and the memorials, publicly subscribed, to the late Prince Consort, were springing up in South Kensington, a spur to Dixon's Shakespearean ambitions.

Dixon edited *The Athenaeum* from January 1853 to August 1869, but his editorial duties did not absorb all his energy. He travelled widely, sometimes accompanying Charles Dilke, the son of *The Athenaeum*'s proprietor Wentworth Dilke. He published travel books and works of scholarship, being an authority on Bacon – his *The Story of Lord Bacon's Life* appeared in 1862. He also helped members of the aristocracy in the ordering of their papers, for instance those of the Duke of Manchester at Kimbolton and, together with Geraldine Jewsbury, those of the indefatigable authoress Lady Morgan.

Assessments of Dixon's character varied greatly, becoming increasingly entrenched as the wrangles over the Tercentenary continued. Regular contributors to *The Athenaeum* such as Geraldine Jewsbury and the novelist, Cordy Jeaffreson, were warm in their personal appreciation, the latter observing in his *A Book of Recollections*: "I never observed anything in his demeanour to other people that gave even a colour of his overbearing temper and demeanour towards professional inferiors."[27]

In contrast Henry Vizetelly, editor of the rival *Illustrated Times*, considered that Dixon "always hungering after notoriety, seeing the chance of a little cheap popularity, joined the movement, and speedily placed himself at its head. It was commonly rumoured that Dixon aspired to the honours of knighthood, and hoped to secure these when matters were ripe."[28]

Whatever his ulterior motive for seizing upon the Tercentenary Celebrations Dixon realised that he was a parvenu in matters Shakespearean and enlisted J O Halliwell as Joint Honorary Secretary of the National Shakespeare Committee. The sequence of letters from Halliwell to Dixon between December 1860 and July 1875 now in the Folger Library reveals the relationship between the two men, especially during the period in which they were working together closely on the Tercentenary. Halliwell was a long-standing reviewer for *The Athenaeum* and early in the 1860s wrote to Dixon of his own schemes in Stratford: "which I hope may do real honour to the memory of Shakespeare, and save us from being inundated by the threatened absurd movements for a monument, statue or mausoleum. The public may at first think there ought to be a Committee, but with previous experience of a birthplace Committee I am convinced that a single individual immediately responsible to public opinion, will best carry it out". (6 November 1861)

Ironically within two and a half years Halliwell allowed himself to be entangled with a committee the primary objective of which was the very type of memorial that he so deeply denigrated. With rare prescience he wrote of his fear that "a very large Committee will be troublesome" (30 June 1863), but for all his misapprehensions meekly connived in Dixon's dominating role: "If you will only act as joint secretary, and tell me exactly the part I am to take, and what to do, I shall go as pleasantly as possible, only it should be *distinctly* understood between us that you are the *directing* secretary". (23 June 1863)

Undoubtedly Dixon needed little persuading to assume such a role and as editor of *The Athenaeum* he was equipped with a ready mouthpiece for his Tercentenary pronouncements. The journal's first pronouncement came on 30 May 1863 when it observed: "As yet we do not hear of any large and inclusive attempt to organise the Shakespeare celebration of next year" and proceeded to outline the need for Royal patronage and the support of learned societies, the universities, the church and, of course, literature and the theatre: "The Committee might be a large one, made to include every sort of celebrity, social, literary and scientific."

In the next issue (6 June) *The Athenaeum* summarised the London parties (The Shakespeare Fund, The Urban Club and The Royal Dramatic College) and their objectives, concluding:

Now it happens, fortunately, that all these objects are legitimate, and might with due subordination, be made to rank in the same general plan. All parties would consent to a statue of Shakespeare being the first thing secured; and no-one would object to any surplus being handed over to the Dramatic College or Shakespeare Fund. We do not think that there would be any great difficulty in either amalgamating the various committees or in harmonising the several projects. Goodwill towards the purpose in view would supply the lubricating kindness of spirit.

The Duke of Manchester took the chair at a meeting of the "Special Shakespeare Committee" at the Royal Society of Literature on 22 June 1863, when it was resolved that a monument should be erected in a conspicuous part of London; that widespread patronage, including that of the Royal Family, should be sought; and that the committee should co-operate with other celebrants at home and abroad. Sir Robert Hamilton was present and supported the monument proposal, though the fact that the Stratford Committee had by then been forced to adopt the same objective meant that from the outset the committees regarded one another in a spirit of rivalry rather than co-operation.

At the end of July *The Athenaeum* announced that "every difficulty which appeared to be in the way of a common understanding and a common action, on the part of those interested in an appropriate celebration of Shakespeare's birthday in April of next year, has now been removed. . . . There is, consequently, now but one body charged before the public with the duty of carrying into visible effect the popular desire that due honour should be done to literature by a monument to Shakespeare."[29]

Apartments were taken at 120 Pall Mall with a clerk present from 10 am to 4 pm and Messrs. Coutts and Co. were appointed bankers, ready to accept the donations which, it was confidently supposed, would flow in.

Plans and Problems

STRATFORD

Though Stratford had been fortunate in its noble patrons (Carlisle, Leigh and Hamilton), the weekly work was conducted by a local committee, usually chaired by Flower, consisting of hoteliers, lawyers, architects, doctors, surgeons, a draper, a grocer, a chemist, the second master at the Grammar School, a Professor of Music (Mr. Mathews) and local actor James Bennett – some thirty men in all. Sub-committees were established for: Finance, Building, Dejeuner, Miscellaneous, Concert, Fancy Dress, General Amusement, Oratorio, Prize Poem, Scholarships, Railway, Address and Advertisement and New Place Gardens. A Site and Memorial Committee was formed later, and on December 9 all the entertainment committees were combined into one.

Flower set a cracking pace, approaching potential patrons and travelling nation-wide seeking support from other municipalities; inevitably "it perhaps looked a little too much like the Committee of one man", but "to those . . . who knew the necessity of the case, and who knew how disinterestedly the man was working . . . almost night and day for months, it would be seen in its true light".[1] Not even Flower could manage without some paid assistance and in August 1863 the Finance Sub-Committee addressed the full committee on "the necessity of a paid Secretary being appointed".[2] Their first choice was not available, and instead Robert Hunter, an Ulsterman then living in the Strand, London, was appointed at a salary of three guineas a week plus travel expenses.

Hunter remains a shadowy figure. Sarah Flower noted that he dined at The Hill on 18 September 1863 and in the following January she commented:

> All very busy now in making preparations for the Shakespeare Tercentenary, which is to be on a grand scale in April. Mr. Hansard staying at The Hill acting as private secretary, and a Mr. Hunter being engaged by the Committee and being very slow – we call them 'The Hare and the Tortoise'.[3]

In spite of the improved communications with the capital (the railway opened in 1860) Stratford was at a disadvantage when it came to negotiating with leading actors and musicians and to overcome this problem it was decided to appoint a London representative in the person of the Revd. John Chippendall Montesquieu Bellew, then the fashionable preacher at Bedford Chapel in New Oxford Street; later a Roman Catholic convert and a highly successful performer reputedly earning £1,000 a year from his Dramatic Readings, "Poetry on Wheels."

Bellew's appearance and manner made him ridiculous in certain eyes:

> The snowy whiteness of his handkerchief is above all praise, his choker is immaculate, his hair is arranged in the most unimpeachable manner, his talent for attitudinising is something marvellous, while his voice has every tone, and, according to need, high or low, mellow or deep, his words are always accompanied with the appropriate music.[4]

But those who knew him better were more sympathetic, Cordy Jeaffreson regarded him as "a much better fellow than his indiscreet tongue caused many people to think of him"[5] and Edmund Yates considered: "Never was a man so wholly and completely his own enemy as Bellew; never did a man so persistently and yet so unintentionally do the wrong thing in the wrong place", continuing:

> He was not very firm, or very strong-minded, or very decisive; but he was frank, kindly, generous, and hospitable, a kind and affectionate husband, an excellent friend and a good father.[6]

The Stratford Committee had ample opportunity to form its own judgement, but initially at least Bellew's credentials were impressive. He was well connected in artistic circles, notably with his near neighbour the French actor Charles Fechter, the conception of whose Hamlet was "much mellowed and improved under the advice of our other friend Bellew".[7] It was with Fechter and Yates that Bellew had visited Granville in 1862 at a time when Bellew, like Halliwell, was interested in New Place, on which he wrote a book *Shakespeare's Home at New Place*, published in 1863.

The title was little more than a pretext for Bellew to broadcast his views on various Shakespearean topics, including the various ways in which the forthcoming Tercentenary might be observed. He covered the gamut of possibilities then in vogue: "the completion of the proposed purchase and the laying-out of New Place Gardens" and the "erection of some monumental structure, commemorative of the purchase and of the 300th celebration of the Poet's Birth, but, while beautiful as a piece of architecture, at the same time a structure that should be practically useful for literary purposes, and a benefit to Stratford and the nation".[8] The idea seemed to owe something to George Dawson's proposal for a Shakespeare Library in Birmingham, first mooted in April 1861. London did not escape Bellew's attention and for them he endorsed "the completion of a Dramatic College . . . wherein childhood and old age may be associated". He saw no need for rivalry or friction and his censure was reserved for Garrick whose "frivolous pageant" was roundly condemned: "A sillier and more useless exhibition was never witnessed", instead the

Tercentenary should concern itself with "the promotion of objects useful to the body of men in connection with whom Shakespeare made his name and fortune".[9]

It was with the body of men and women who currently brought forth Shakespeare's immortal characters that Bellew was to be concerned on behalf of the Stratford Committee. The Committee set its sights high and invited Fanny Kemble, Helen Faucit, Ben Webster, Samuel Phelps and Charles Fechter, not one of whom appeared in Stratford. The problem was that, unlike 1769, there was no undisputed leader of the theatrical profession. Macready was in retirement. Phelps had given up his management of Sadler's Wells and was considered out-of-date by many. The Keans had ended their management at the Princess's Theatre and were in Australia. Fechter enjoyed a fashionable, but rather ephemeral success; Irving's star was yet to rise. Of actresses Fanny Kemble would be abroad and Helen Faucit was pre-occupied with her ranking and respectability as the wife of Theodore Martin, the late Prince Consort's biographer. All were jealous of their professional reputation and over-reactive to any suspected slight to their dignity. In such circumstances much depended upon individual value judgements and personal contacts.

The relationship between Phelps and Fechter was such that any enterprise hoping to include them both was almost certainly doomed to failure. Phelps was immensely proud of his Shakespearean record at Sadler's Wells where, between 1844 and 1860, he had produced all the plays save *King Richard II, Troilus and Cressida, Titus Andronicus* and *Henry VI* for a total of 1,632 performances, 171 as Hamlet. The contrast between Phelps's and Fechter's style has been summarised by Shirley Allen:

> It seems clear that Phelps's delivery appeared to be slow and measured to the critics of the late fifties because they had become accustomed to the new style of rapid and conversational delivery. Fechter's appearance as Hamlet in 1861 was the greatest single event in this evolution from the traditional to the modern school of acting . . . by ignoring stage convention, Fechter freed English actors from bondage to the past and established the principle of innovation in acting Shakespeare.[10]

In spite of this incipient rivalry Phelps unwisely joined Fechter's management at the Lyceum, contracted to give three performances a week for twelve months from 1 January 1863. After three months Phelps had not appeared once and the crunch came when *Hamlet* was announced. Phelps naively assumed that he would play Hamlet and on being informed that he was to be the Ghost retorted: "You thought that I would play the Ghost to your Hamlet – yours! Well, d – n your impudence!"[11] It was many years before John Coleman, who claimed that Fechter "had an unfortunate knack of scratching everyone the wrong way",[12] engineered a meeting between the two actors at Charles Reade's house at which they became reconciled.

It fell to Hunter to make the first overture to Phelps, which he did in a letter dated 7 December 1863, enclosing a copy of the committee's resolution "that the Secretary be instructed to write to Samuel Phelps, Esq., requesting that gentleman to take part in the Dramatic Performances at Stratford-upon-Avon in April next".[13] He added a private letter alluding to Hamlet, Othello and Macbeth. Phelps replied that he was committed to perform at Drury Lane on 23 April, to which Hunter, answered that "*Hamlet* will be played on Tuesday the 26 of that month", advised him that Bellew would call "to see you on the subject, and will probably do so on Monday next".[14]

Since an invitation had also been extended to Fechter, whose only creditable Shakespearean role was Hamlet, it is evident that Hunter had no authority for specifying that part or any other to Phelps at this stage. Bellew, unaware of Hunter's misplaced initiative, delayed his visit to Phelps and pressed Fechter's case in a letter to Flower dated 12 December:

> Phelps is a wretched Hamlet, but he is an Englishman. Fechter is a very attractive Hamlet, but he is (as Mr. Phelps called him) "that bloody Frenchman"! – I shall not approach Phelps until I hear from you, but let me hear as quickly as possible.
>
> I believe if we could get him to play Hamlet, he would be an *immense attraction*. Phelps would be none at all. I should say Mr. Phelps never has made any mark in Hamlet; and he is now quite too old.[15]

So over Christmas Bellew stalled and Phelps grew impatient, until Flower received Fechter's enthusiastic reply, dated December 28: "Hamlet sera trop heureux de fêter la naissance de son immortal createur, ne parler donc ni de peine donnée, ni de sacrifice d'argent".[16] Fechter's Hamlet settled, Bellew proceeded to inform Phelps of the committee's plans in more detail:

> I have delayed writing to you until I could know definitely what Play of Shakespeare's the Committee proposed to present.
>
> It is now arranged that "Cymbeline" will be produced . . . on the evening of Tuesday, April 26th. . . . I should think the Programme incomplete unless both you and Miss Faucit could be included in it.[17]

Phelps now unleashed his formidable capacity for indignation, asserting that Hunter had offered him Hamlet and that was the only part he wished to play. The hapless Bellew dispatched a letter to Phelps, protesting "perfect ignorance regarding Mr. Hunter's letter to you or who directed him to specify 'Hamlet', 'Macbeth', or 'Othello'"[18] and another to Flower surmising: "Phelps may well feel annoyed. What I hope is the truth, is, that Mr. Hunter wrote on his own authority, naming those plays and that all *he had authority* to do was *simply to invite Phelps* to perform".[19]

The acrimony smouldered on, Phelps wrote to Flower, claiming the right "to be considered the foremost man in my profession in a demonstration meant to honour Shakespeare" and asserting: "The Stratford Committee have insulted me by asking any man in this country to play *Hamlet* on such an occasion without having first offered the character to [me]".[20]

Flower was courteous but unmoved by Phelps's protest and threat to publish the correspondence, which he did – in part – even on the cover of the Drury Lane programme.

Although the fault was Hunter's, much of the blame was attached to Bellew and, after another unsuccessful negotiation with Benjamin Webster, the Entertainment Committee resolved on 22 February: "That Mr. Bellew be requested not to make any more arrangements on behalf of the Committee until further communicated with". The full Committee confirmed on 2 March that: "Mr. Bellew be requested to desist from acting further on behalf of the Committee".[21]

Bellew's departure coincided with that of his adversary Hunter. In February 1864 Hunter's deputy David Edwards, dismissed for opening certain letters during Hunter's absence, reacted by alleging professional and financial misconduct by Hunter. This, together with the Phelps affair, was enough to lose Hunter his job, though he still wrote his record of the Stratford Tercentenary in a private capacity. James Bennett took over Bellew's duties in London and Dr. Kingsley resumed the Honorary Secretaryship.

Bennett found that there was widespread hostility to Fechter's prominence in the Stratford programme and this hampered his negotiations. In spite of its treatment of Fechter's advocate, Bellew, the Stratford Committee remained loyal to the actor: "In fact the Committee, as honour bound, stuck to Mr. Fechter through good and evil report. Old King Duncan did not place in Cawdor who betrayed him a trust more absolute".[22]

To begin with, all went well. In February Fechter visited Stratford and suggested various alterations in the Pavilion which was then under construction. It was not until late March, only a month before the festival, that "Humph" Barnett, Fechter's Acting Manager, wrote to Kingsley stating that Fechter would withdraw because the dismissal of Bellew gave "the face of truth to the false and injurious statement . . . that Mr. Fechter by under-current and trickery ways, forced on the choice of his Hamlet".[23] Sarah Flower believed that "Mr. Bellew . . . persuaded Fechter to throw up his engagement"[24], but such vindictiveness seems as unlikely in Bellew as would such loyalty in Fechter and a more likely explanation was given by the latter: "I find the general public turning against me".[25] National resentment that a Frenchman should take the leading role in celebrating England's greatest poet had been increased by what was seen to be the shabby treatment of Phelps, and Fechter, who was genuinely unwell, must have feared for his reception in Stratford.

Whatever Fechter's reason the Stratford Committee's dilemma was acute. It even approached Phelps, who was surprisingly sympathetic until

Falconer, to whom he was contracted at Drury Lane, refused his permission. Frederick Ledger, editor of *The Era*, suggested James Anderson from the Surrey Theatre, who was preparing a production of *Henry VI Part ii*, but it was John Baldwin Buckstone of the Haymarket whom the Revds. G Granville and J C Young (son of the actor and Vicar of Ilmington) and Dr. Kingsley visited for advice. He was already bringing his *Twelfth Night*, but a message came from George Vining, who had established a management at the Princess's after falling out with Fechter at the Lyceum, offering *The Comedy of Errors*. This abridged version was judged to be too slight, but then:

> Mr. Vining kindly offered to proceed to Paris and ascertain whether Mdlle Stella Colas would consent to personate Juliet in the tragedy which drew such houses in London some months since during the lady's engagement at the Princess's.[26]

Success attended Vining's mission, but Stella Colas' letters to Dr. Kingsley indicate her apprehension at the likely chauvinist reaction "on the subject of foreigners bearing a prominent part in this public homage to the national poet" and she insisted that should any misunderstandings arise "I shall trust to your promise to do as you propose, to publish the letters that have passed between us on the matter."[27] Misunderstandings did arise, not with the public, but with the profession, notably Helen Faucit.

After Phelps's refusal to act in *Cymbeline*, Helen Faucit agreed to Rosalind in *As You Like It*. Theodore Martin busied himself on his wife's behalf, maintaining, improbably, that she objected to the casting of her kinsman Walter Farren as Orlando and checking her dressing room in Stratford. Whilst Helen Faucit no longer coveted Juliet, her (or more significantly her husband's) pride was offended by the prospect of a French actress appearing in a role which she had once made her own. Theodore Martin was adamant: if Mlle Colas appeared, his wife would not. Faced with the choice between Rosalind or Juliet Buckstone counselled Juliet on the basis that without Mlle Colas, Vining's *Romeo and Juliet* could not be mounted whereas a substitute Rosalind, Mrs. Hermann Vezin, was available.

Although drama was to be the centrepiece of the programme (unlike Garrick's when no play was performed), music was also an important part. Initially Bellew took responsibility for booking singers, approaching Madame Titiens for the inevitable Handel oratorio. Bellew was replaced by Alfred Mellon; Birmingham born, married to actress Sarah Woolgar, he was successively musical director at the Haymarket and Adelphi Theatres, and the English Opera at Covent Garden. He accepted the post with enthusiasm "Nothing in the world would give me greater pleasure"[28], and set about it with determination and a sense of humour. The latter he needed. He discovered the frailty of Bellew's understanding with Titiens, but "I have already succeeded in getting Lemmens-Sherrington in place of Titiens".[29] Such optimism proved misplaced, for Mme. Sherrington's husband exhibited the same proprietorial chauvinism as Theodore Martin: "I am sorry to say I cannot allow Madame L Sherrington to accept being a substitute to a foreigner's refusal".[30]

Madame Sainton-Dolby was engaged instead but she was prevented from appearing by last minute illness and Miss Louisa Baxter stood in. Sims Reeves took some pinning down, but for once his health held out. As well as booking artists, Mellon busied himself with a range of activities from composing special settings to fixing travel passes for musicians and making special arrangements for the transport of large instruments. Furthermore his irreverent jibes at Bellew and Fechter must have fortified the Flowers:

I saw Barnett yesterday and bade him convey a large *quantity of pepper* to Fechter with my love.[31]

LONDON

To Hepworth Dixon the key to success lay in recruiting notables to his National Shakespeare Committee. *The Athenaeum* blazoned forth the names of the illustrious: two Dukes, nine Earls, a Viscount, three Bishops, nine Lords, six baronets plus Right Honourables, Generals, Reverends and the flower of literary and theatrical London. Patrons were, of course, expected to contribute to the funds, but in London as in Stratford there were those who actually paid and those who asked to be "put down" for so much. The published lists of donations made no distinction between the two categories, and small contributors, who usually paid up, resented being put in an unfavourable light by what seemed more generous donors. This practice also made it virtually impossible for either Committee to budget with any accuracy.

Dixon's hopes of Royal patronage were not realised, probably because the National Shakespeare Committee never inspired complete confidence, so the Duke of Manchester became President, his main qualification apparently being his friendship with Dixon. In these circumstances great store was set upon the recruitment of Vice-Presidents and Dickens and Sir Edward Bulwer Lytton were invited and accepted. The next obvious candidate was Thackeray, but between him and *The Athenaeum* there existed a long-standing mutual antipathy which had deepened at the time of the 1863 celebrations of Shakespeare's birthday.

Thackeray's unfortunate marriage made him depend upon the clubland of London for companionship, and the importance he attached to it was illustrated by his insistence that Edmund Yates's membership of the Garrick should be terminated following his unflattering article on Thackeray in the second issue of *Town Talk* (12 June 1858). Thackeray also frequented Evans's Supper Rooms where Douglas Jerrold, the brothers Mayhew, Landseer, Sala, Dickens, Yates and Jeaffreson were often to be seen in the genial surroundings, presided over by "Paddy" Green, which

Thackeray recaptured as the main source for the "Cave of Harmony" in *The Newcomes*. Next door to Evans's was Clunn's Hotel on the first floor of which the meetings of "Our Club" were held.

"Our Club" was founded in 1860 by Douglas Jerrold with a membership including Shirley Brooks, Dr. Doran, Ben Webster, Hepworth Dixon and Cordy Jeaffreson. Thackeray joined in November 1861 and formed a particular affection for "Little Hamstede" the club's deformed secretary. The highlight of the club year was the annual Shakespeare dinner which was held on the Saturday following 23 April – in deference to the Garrick Club which celebrated on the birthday itself. The speaker on 25 April 1863 was William Makepeace Thackeray. After-dinner speeches were not Thackeray's forte, but this one was to be one of his unhappiest.

The Athenaeum of that day carried a review of a novel, *The Story of Elizabeth*, by his daughter Anne, whose literary career began in 1860 at the age of 23 when she published *Little Scholars* in her father's *Cornhill Magazine*. The reviewer conceded that the novel was "undeniably clever", but it "turns on a subject which is, or ought to be, quite inadmissible for a novel: the antagonism of a mother and daughter, both rivals for the love of the same man".[32] The review was anonymous, but as Thackeray left the table after his speech, he bowed slightly and stiffly to Jeaffreson "whilst Shirley Brooks regarded me (Jeaffreson) with a look of exultation, which I could not at the moment account for".[33] The reason soon became clear: Thackeray assumed that Jeaffreson had written the review.

The convention of the day forbade Jeaffreson from disclaiming the article since that would incriminate someone else. So bitter did the dispute become that Sir Wentworth Dilke absolved Jeaffreson from this rule, but the novelist felt obliged to keep silence; eventually Thackeray was disabused, probably by the reviewer herself, Geraldine Jewsbury. Irrespective of the authorship, Thackeray's hostility towards *The Athenaeum* and its editor was irremediable and inevitably extended towards the National Shakespeare Committee in which Dixon and now Jeaffreson were so active. Cordy Jeaffreson, as one of the General Secretaries, was responsible for issuing the invitation to Thackeray to become a Vice-President though he thought that Thackeray "was not likely to give his countenance to the undertaking in which Hepworth Dixon, the editor of *The Athenaeum,* figured as . . . the chief projector of the enterprise".[34]

Jeaffreson's inclination was to let matters rest, but he was instructed by the Committee to invite Thackeray again whilst Dixon was away visiting the Holy Land, in the forlorn hope that he might accept "when the editor of *The Athenaeum* was out of the country".[35] Still there was no response and at the Committee meeting on 8 December 1863 Henry Vizetelly proposed that Thackeray should be appointed as a Vice-President. Colonel Sykes, in the chair, was about to declare this passed *nem con* when Dixon interposed to the effect that as Thackeray was not an ordinary member of the Committee he was ineligible to be a Vice-President, a technicality which seemed to have been overlooked in previous cases.

Accounts of what happened next vary. "The Lounger in the Club" in Vizetelly's *Illustrated Times* recounted that "a novelist of feeble powers took it upon himself to say that he had reasons for believing Mr. Thackeray thought himself so immeasurably superior to the individuals comprising the general committee that he would decline to join it".[36] The novelist in question, Jeaffreson, recalled:

> I told the Committee in the fewest possible words my reasons for thinking it would be unwise for them to trouble Mr. Thackeray at that juncture with a third request that he would join in a movement from which he thought it right to hold himself aloof.[37]

Whatever the tone of Jeaffreson's contribution – reasonable or vindictive – the Committee took a vote and out of the sixty present only nine – or in some counts thirteen – voted for Thackeray. Thackeray's friends planned to press his case at the next meeting, but fate intervened for on the morning of Christmas Eve the novelist was found dead in his bed, and overnight the affair became one of life and death. Amongst his papers were found accounts of the proceedings in the national press – the great man's last reading matter.

What Thackeray had stipulated should be an unostentatious funeral at Kensal Green cemetery attracted over 2,000 mourners. They witnessed the novelist's two daughters looking into the open grave with a grief that was touching to behold. Cordy Jeaffreson cannot have been alone in wondering whether the "notorious review . . . may perhaps be regarded as one of several indirect causes of Thackeray's death".[38]

The monthly meeting of the National Shakespeare Committee on 4 January was awaited with great expectation. A motion was passed regretting that "untoward circumstances should have occurred to prevent the enrolment of his name on the list of Vice-Presidents"[39]; then Dixon rose and, after weeping crocodile tears, moved "that all record of the circumstances be erased from the minute book of the National Shakespeare Committee".[40] What Dixon hoped to achieve is puzzling since the incident was already so widely known, but the suggestion served to galvanise opposition and not only the proposal, but the Committee's whole report, was rejected at the instigation of Theodore Martin.

Martin wrested the initiative from Dixon and together with the Revd. Dr. Vaughan, Tom Taylor and Shirley Brooks, was charged with the task of preparing a new address setting forth the Committee's objectives. The task proved to be impossible and on 20 January *The Times* published their letter of resignation, which made more general criticism of the Committee's work:

> Without dwelling upon the irregular and unbusiness-like character of the proceedings of the executive body, the undersigned complained that more than half-a-year has been wasted in procuring a list of names, which would have been given in without solicitation, had a practical and worthy scheme been laid before the public.[41]

"The Thunderer" now threw its weight behind Stratford: "Our sympathy, in so far as we have any sympathy with the movement, goes to Stratford". A more scurrilous journal published a parody beginning:

"Who killed HA'P'ORTH DIXON?"
"Who killed Ha'p'orth Dixon?"
"I" said T Martin
"Of that I am sartin
"I killed Ha'p'orth Dixon . . ."[42]

The National Shakespeare Committee tried to salvage what it could, and *The Athenaeum* announced a restructuring as a result of which: "every resolution was adopted without a dissenting voice".[43] However, the Committee still failed to present a convincing programme of events and although *The Athenaeum* announced that the lessees of Drury Lane, Covent Garden, the Haymarket, the Princess's, the Adelphi and the Lyceum had promised Shakespearean performances it was evident that these would take place without the ministrations of the Committee.

The pressing need to arrange some distinctive commemorative events may explain the decision to send G Linnaeus Banks (one of the Dramatic Secretaries, a journalist by profession, who maintained a keen interest in Friendly Societies and Mechanics' Institutes) to a meeting of the Trades' Provisional Committee at the Whittington Club (in the Strand) in early March. This organisation included representatives of such trades as bookbinders (Mr. Dunning), engineers (Mr. Allen), coachmakers (Mr. Webb), painters (Mr. Medland) with Mr. Odgers (secretary of the London Trades Council). Two resolutions were passed to the effect that "the objects contemplated by the National Shakespeare Committee are entitled to the warm sympathy of the working classes of the United Kingdom" and "a Committee be appointed . . . to communicate with the operatives throughout the kingdom to raise subscriptions to the Memorial".[44]

The Working Men's Shakespeare Committee now took a lead in promoting certain arrangements: a concert at the Royal Agricultural Hall, Islington and a tree-planting ceremony on Primrose Hill. The Queen herself agreed to donate an oak from the Royal Forest, Windsor, and Samuel Phelps consented to perform the planting ceremony. William Cowper MP, a member of the National Shakespeare Committee and Commissioner of Works, gave permission for the oak to be ceremoniously planted on Primrose Hill.

A project which appeared to encompass harmoniously monarch, government and all classes of people, concealed a deeper purpose based on political dissent and agitation, as a report of the Working Men's Committee meeting in mid-April revealed: "The Sub-Committee brought up an amended programme of the proceedings on the 23rd inst. rendered necessary by the Government refusing the use of the Parks for the purpose of the demonstration. . . . It was also resolved that General Garibaldi should be invited to attend at the Agricultural Hall in the evening, and Messrs. Odgers and Cremer were deputed to see the General for that purpose."[45]

The National Shakespeare Committee had begun as a pillar of establishment respectability. Now, ironically, it found itself sheltering a movement which sought to use the Tercentenary for promulgating its political views, especially on the visit to England of the Italian politician and soldier, General Giuseppe Garibaldi.

The Pavilion

The need to erect a building in Stratford for the festival was recognised early on. The Stratford committee included builders and architects, and a Building Sub-Committee was formed with the task of preparing a brief. The presence on that committee of the architects Thompson and Colbourne, who were to design the Pavilion, ensured that the building corresponded closely with what was needed. Outline drawings were ready by September:

> Your Building Committee having taken into consideration the different purposes for which a Building required for the celebration of the above Festival is to be used viz – Dejeuner, Concerts, Dramatic Representations, Balls, etc. recommend the erection of a Building capable of accommodating upwards of Five Thousand Persons shewn by the accompanying drawings which they consider the best arrangement that can be adopted.[1]

Mr. T Mason offered the use of a paddock in Southern Lane, reassuringly on the far side from the river. The site was later marked by a line of poplars planted by Sarah Flower,[2] though they no longer survive. Hunter was charged with seeking tenders which were received by mid-November. Four were submitted: Sample and Co., Gloucester £2,449; George Clarke and Sons, Wootton Wawen £1,799; J Cox and Son £1,475; and Branson and Murray, Birmingham £1,300. J Cox jnr. of the local building firm was of course on the Committee, but when the tenders came up for discussion he proposed the acceptance of Branson and Murray's estimate, an unselfish act which the Committee may have regretted later as their wrangles with the Birmingham company dragged on.

The local architects, Thompson and Colbourne, can have had no previous experience of designing a building like the Pavilion in which they achieved an original synthesis of form and function comparable with that of Paxton's Crystal Palace. A possible prototype might have been the more substantial buildings erected for itinerant circuses: like many of them the Pavilion was wooden on masonry foundations, but the time (five months) and scale (12,000 cubic feet of timber; 12 tons of wrought iron; and upwards of four tons of nails) of its construction imply an altogether more elaborate edifice. The builders, Branson and Murray, were specialists in railway construction. With hindsight it is tempting to see similarities with circular engine-turning sheds such as that at Chalk Farm, now converted into the Roundhouse (1847, Stephenson, Dockray and Normanville), but the architects' designs would have been independent of the awarding of the contract and Branson and Murray's woefully inaccurate tender does not suggest that their particular expertise was relevant. Another resemblance is to the Chichester Festival Theatre, which was constructed almost exactly one hundred years after the Pavilion.

Certainly the Pavilion was sufficiently unusual to attract widespread attention in the press, which produced internal and external drawings, ground-plans and detailed descriptions. The basic shape of the Pavilion was a dodecagon:

> It is in the form of a regular dodecagon, being as near an approach to a perfect amphitheatre as the mechanical arrangements of the materials (all timber) used in its construction would permit. Internally there are nine faces of the figure perfect; the first and the eleventh are halved by the twelfth being advanced more to the front, and thus a fine opening is obtained for the stage. There are two tiers of boxes, one of them being on the same level with the arena, or pit.[3]

The stage (1 on the diagram) was 74 ft. wide, by 56 ft. deep, giving a proscenium opening of 31 ft. with a height of 25 ft. The stage-front had been brought forward in a semi-circle at Fechter's suggestion. These dimensions were generous by the standards of theatres of the day and must have aided the storing of the scenery brought down from London. The fitting up of the stage was supervised by Mr. Wales, stage carpenter of the Haymarket Theatre, and the curtain, executed and donated by Telbin, resembled that at the Princess's Theatre: a representation of a statue of Shakespeare in a sort of draped vestibule with Holy Trinity in the background and with two white satin curtains looped up in the top corners to relieve the otherwise rich colouring. The proscenium (by O'Connor of the Haymarket Theatre) was uncompromisingly massive and, one on each side, were two allegorical figures representing "Genius" and "Immortality". Telbin estimated his normal charge for such a curtain at £60–£70 exclusive of roller and fittings, but ventured that "after having been used on such a memorable occasion as the Stratford Festival it ought at any rate to fetch no less a sum than I have mentioned".[4]

The northern focus of the Pavilion was the stage; the southern was the orchestra (2 on diagram), which was capable of holding 530 performers. Thus for the musical offerings the audience faced the opposite way, though the large area devoted to the orchestra was not wasted at other events, it could be removed, thereby levelling off the auditorium, or covered over. For the banquet on the first day it was the location of the high table: "This afternoon the front of the movable orchestra, which stands at the back of the salle, and consequently faces the stage, was occupied by the table of honour assigned to the President and more distinguished guests, who were thus raised on a dais of unusual elevation".[5] Eight other tables stretched across the floor at right angles to

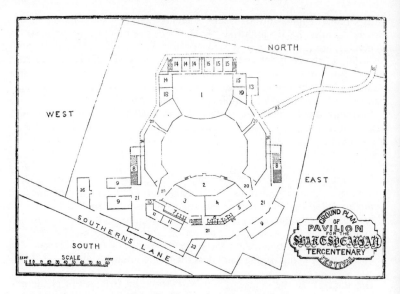

EXPLANATION OF GROUND PLAN OF PAVILION

 1 The Stage.
 2 Lower part of the Orchestra, removed during theatrical performances and ball.
 3 Gentlemen's Retiring Room during oratorio and ball, but used for spectators during the theatrical representations.
 4 Ladies' ditto, ditto, ditto.
 5 Retiring Room.
 6 Ladies.
 7 Gentlemen.
 8 Stairs to Gallery.
 9 Refreshment Rooms.
10 Offices for Opera Glasses.
11 Cloak Rooms.
12 Stairs to Orchestra.
13 Committee Room.
14 Ladies' Dressing Rooms.
15 Gentlemen's Dressing Rooms.
16 Stairs to Ladies' Dressing Rooms.
17 Stairs to Gentlemen's ditto.
18 Green Room.
19 General Dressing Room.
20 Entrance to Ground Floor of Building.
21 Covered Vestibule and Corridors to various entrances of building.
22 Carriage Platform.
23 Office for Sale and Exchange of Tickets.
24 Covered Way.
25 Church Street Approach to Pavilion.
26 Burton and Son's Photographic Studio.

the top table, and further tables were on the stage (for the "professionals" who were thus kept in their proper place, complete with the set for *Twelfth Night* to make them feel at home) and in the lower boxes. At the banquet and the ball the upper boxes were used for non-participating onlookers "stamped with an expression of weariness and disgust".[6]

Although the Pavilion was reversible, the acoustics were equally good each way round: "it seems as though a voice would be heard throughout the whole of the Pavilion with unusual ease".[7] The sight-lines were also excellent. The ground-level auditorium, which had to be flat to accommodate the dancing and eating, offered uninterrupted views when used for performances. The Pavilion's capacity was round 5,000: 2,000 on chairs in the pit and 3,000 on benches equally divided between the pit and the low gallery. The 2,000 chairs were of course the top-price seats at 21s. for the

MR. E. F. FLOWER, THE MAYOR OF STRATFORD.

Edward Fordham Flower,
mayor of Stratford-upon-Avon

MASTER OF ONE OF THE 'THREE Rs.'

The Rev. J C M Bellew,
London representative of the Stratford Committee

A ribbon manufactured in Coventry to mark the Stratford celebrations

The exterior of the Stratford Pavilion

The Banquet at the Pavilion

The Solemn Temple ← → The Great Globe itself ←— Yea all which it inherit—ɔЄ

The Moral Lord Mayor

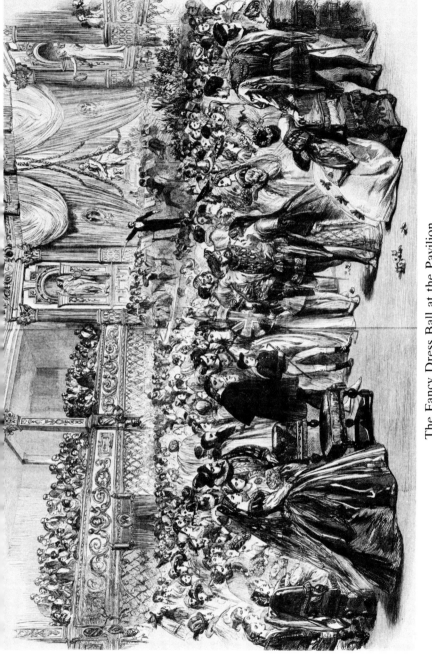

The Fancy Dress Ball at the Pavilion

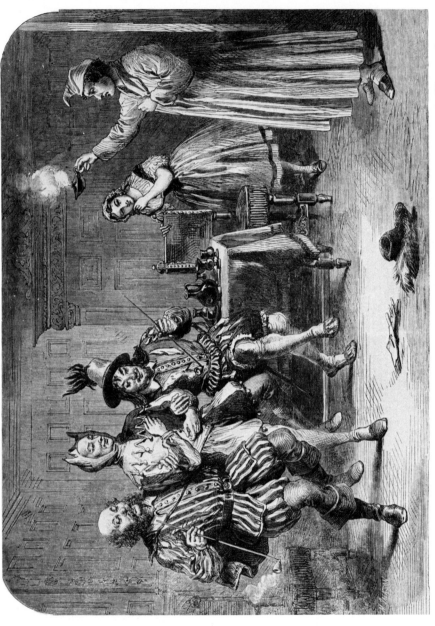

Twelfth Night as performed at the Pavilion by the company from the Theatre Royal Haymarket

plays and *The Messiah*; 10s. 6d. for the Miscellaneous Concert. Gallery places could also be reserved in advance—10s.6d. and 5s. respectively—and unreserved places, presumably the benches at the back of the stalls from which the sight-lines would not have been too good, the floor being level, were priced at 5s. and 2s. 6d. respectively.

The fact that the Pavilion was constructed of wood did not mean that it was a rough-hewn Globe-like structure. The ambiance was closer to the red-plush of the West End theatres. The lighting was a particular feature. The Pavilion was surmounted by a lantern, the top of which was 74 ft. above the ground. The lower part of the lantern was made of zinc to aid ventilation. Inside, a splendid gasolier or corona with 320 jets was suspended from the centre to provide the main source of light for evening performances. The stage was equipped with a sophisticated system of wing, batten and foot lights.

The firm of Charles Brothers of Leamington Spa won the contract for the internal decoration of the building at a cost of £300, though that was considerably exceeded. The style was considered to be Elizabethan: "An ingenious monogram of Shakespeare's name formed a prominent feature in the beautifully painted canvas on the back wall. The front of the boxes was decorated with scroll work, interspersed with Shakespearean medallions and quotations. . . ."[8] Thousands of chairs had to be acquired and, although they had to be re-arranged and stored as needed, the best-placed at least were draped in scarlet cloth, with cushioned seats covered with silk velvet.

All this cost more than anticipated, to the original estimate of £1,300 Branson and Murray added a staggering £2,052 19s. 11d. The committee protested and the dispute went to the arbitration of William Thompson, of Grantham, and William Richard Grittens, an architect of Westminster, who determined that £1,763 10s. 7d. was a fair price for the extra work.[9] Decorations increased by £138 7s. 11d., the architects' fees came to £122 15s. 10d. and all in all, including a dinner for the workers presided over by Edward Flower, the Pavilion cost £4,446 10s. 7d.,[10] a major element in the final deficit.

However, there is no doubt that the Pavilion was quite literally the foundation of the festival's success. It performed all the tasks demanded of it and was widely praised by locals and visitors alike; Andrew Halliday considered it "a model of what a theatre ought to be . . . a great achievement and too much praise cannot be awarded to the committee. . . ."[11] It was ironic that whilst the Tercentenary committees failed to erect a permanent memorial, this temporary structure should have been so signally successful. It must have been a sadness to those concerned to see it removed, but the site was only temporarily available and any money that could be recouped from its sale was badly needed.

The auction, conducted by Messrs. Puttick and Simpson of Leicester Square, took place on 31 May and included everything from Telbin's "New Act Drop" to O'Connor's "Elegant Proscenium", the "New Gas Fittings" and 2,300 "stained birchwood cane seated chairs" to hair-brushes, scrubbing-brushes, watering cans, "a wash leather" and a rather demoralising 1,700 copies of the official programme.[12] The sale realised only a paltry £375 15s. 10d. and many a member of the theatrical profession snapped up a bargain that day at Stratford's expense. Telbin's beautiful act drop with all the fittings went to Mr. Shepherd of the Surrey Theatre for a mere £26 instead of the £60–£70 normally charged; and O'Connor's proscenium to the Amphitheatre, Leeds for 6 guineas. A Mr. Clapham, also of Leeds, got the corona for 56 shillings, and the rest of the gas fittings were knocked down to Shepherd for £3 15s. It was a discreditable end to a noble edifice.

The Stratford Festival

Inexorably the great day approached. 23 April that year was a Saturday, which although still a working day for many, meant that more people were free to participate in the celebrations, if they wished, than on an ordinary weekday. A proposal by the National Shakespeare Committee for a public holiday came to nought.

April 23

The Stratford proceedings started at noon with the President and Committee proceeding from the Town Hall to "inspect the site fixed upon for the erection of the National Memorial, at the Market House, in High Street".[1] Fortunately the festival quickly rose above this pedestrian opening. The main event of the first day was the Banquet at three o'clock in the Pavilion, catered for by Mr. Mountford of Worcester and attended by over 700, plus "spectators, who looked on with all the gratification that is to be derived from witnessing enjoyments which one is not permitted to share".[2] It cost 5s. to have one's appetite whetted, 21s. to have it satisfied.

The attention to detail was meticulous: an appropriate ornament decked each table; the knife handles were engraved with Shakespeare's head and the bonbons were similarly decorated; each dish was accompanied by an appropriate textual quotation. There were fifteen toasts, all proposed and twelve responded to. The Earl of Carlisle was surprisingly nervous, but asserted the propriety of the occasion: "As I think it is right that such a celebration should be held, I am not less clear that the right place to hold it should be Stratford-upon-Avon".[3]

Lord Shrewsbury invoked his kinship with the Talbots; Lord Houghton gave an accomplished and witty speech; William Creswick, the only actor to speak, got rather carried away with highflown rhetoric. The most unusual contribution was an address by Professor Leitner on behalf of the Hochstift, the foundation which had purchased Goethe's house, and a further international flavour was added by telegrams from the Imperial University of Moscow and from Kharhov in Southern Russia, though the latter raised speculation about a possible hoax.

Notwithstanding the eminence of the visitors, Stratford had a worthy spokesman in Edward Flower. Physically he was an impressive figure with "his fine, strongly-marked features, and his luxuriant white hair and beard, looking more like a patrician burgomaster of the late 16th and 17th century, even still more like a Doge of Venice, when the Doge was a Doge indeed, than a Mayor of the 19th century".[4] He began, disingenuously but humorously, by saying: "We have all of us been too busy doing, and have had no time to think of words",[5] but he was wise enough to keep his contribution short, dwelling mainly on the German Hochstift.

The schedule for the 1864 festival was not as compressed as Garrick's Jubilee but there remained "A Grand Display of Fireworks by Mr. Darby, the Celebrated Pyrotechnist" at 9 pm, including the ascent of two balloons, one emblazoned "Shakespeare", the other "Stratford-on-Avon", each discharging "an unique and beautiful Aerial display" and costing in all £86 19s. Andrew Halliday, the dramatist and contributor to Dickens's *All the Year Round*, having attended the tree-planting ceremony on Primrose Hill in London, arrived as the fireworks were getting under way and sought the Birthplace:

> A few more steps and I was in front of the House, and I saw it for the first time by the light of fireworks! The thrill did not rise. By the garish light of red, and blue and green fires I saw a house that had been restored out of all its antiquity.[6]

April 24

The Sunday was devoted to church-going at Holy Trinity, where the Revd. G Granville presided over large congregations at 11 am and 3 pm. The preacher at morning service was Dr. Richard Chenevix Trench, who had been consecrated as Archbishop of Dublin in January of that year for a term of office which was to encompass Gladstone's dis-establishment of the Church of Ireland, which Trench strongly opposed. Trench was an apt choice in many respects apart from his obvious allegiance to Carlisle; he was a distinguished Biblical scholar, philologist – the instigator of the Oxford English Dictionary –, translator from Spanish, and a poet in his own right, having been a contemporary of Alfred Tennyson and Arthur Hallam at Cambridge and a member of the Apostles with them. He was also, alas, of a notoriously retiring disposition, a quality which led to some exasperation with his sermon. Sarah Flower complained: "The Shakespeare sermon preached by Archbishop Trench, but he had so bad a delivery that those a little way off could only catch the word Shakespeare – which rather shocked them".[7] Andrew Halliday, ensconced opposite the poet's bust in the chancel, concurred: "Every now and then, however, I hear the word 'Shakespeare'".[8]

Trench's sermon was widely reported, for the benefit of posterity as well as the hard of hearing, and provides an object lesson in the Victorian establishment's desire to use Shakespeare to reinforce its own moral, social and political outlook. His text was "Every good gift and every perfect gift is from above and cometh down from the Father of Light", the first verse of the day's Epistle (*St. James I.* v. 17). The text itself implied the Archbishop's first point that gifts such as Shakespeare's were God-given. He then addressed himself to why the poet's tercentenary should be celebrated and conceded that if literature were "merely an amusement" there would be no justification, but Shakespeare's work entertained

without corrupting and furthermore instilled valuable precepts in its
readers.

By it the mighty heart of a people may be animated and quickened to
heroic enterprise and worthiest endeavour. Those who should thus
mould a nation's life should be men acquainted with God's scheme of
the universe, cheerfully working in their own appointed sphere the
work which has been assigned to them, accepting God's world
because it is His, with all its strange riddles and infinite perplexities,
with all the burdens which it lays upon each one of us, not fiercely
dashing and shaking themselves like imprisoned birds against the bars
of a prison-house, or moodily nourishing in their own hearts and in
the hearts of others thoughts of discontent, revolt and despair. Such a
poet I am bold to affirm we possess in Shakespeare.[9]

Dr. Trench proceeded to extol "those ideals of perfect womanhood
which are the loveliest, perhaps the most transcendent creations of his
art", dwelling in particular on Imogen and Miranda and perforce omitting
other less accommodating examples. King John was cited for his treatment of "the pretensions of a Roman bishop", and Cordelia as an
example of Shakespeare's moral purpose, bringing a trail of sorrows upon
herself.

The morning service did not finish until 2 pm, leaving scant time for
anything beyond spiritual sustenance for those who were also attending
the 3 pm service. Then the preacher was Dr. Charles Wordsworth, Bishop
of St. Andrews and nephew of the Lakeland poet. In that year he
published *On Shakespeare's Knowledge and Use of the Bible* and later
edited a twelve-volume edition of the plays. An Harrovian contemporary
of Trench's, he was an altogether more prepossessing figure, tall with
brown curly hair and a winning smile. He took as his text: "All Thy Works
Praise Thee, O Lord" (*Psalms* 145, v. 10). Over £100 was collected
towards the chancel fund at the two services.

In the evening the hospitable Flowers entertained distinguished guests
at The Hill.

April 25
With the weekend over, visitors had access to a range of attractions,
official and unofficial. The discerning naturally wanted to see the buildings
associated with Shakespeare's life and *The Times* considered that these
were well presented:

Everything is done here to facilitate the investigation of the antiqu-
ary. The museum in Shakespeare's birthplace is exhibited by a lady
who knows all about the things to which she directs attention, and
this stands in remarkable contrast to the tribes of exhibitors, both in
England and on the continent. Similar commendation may be
bestowed upon the lady who inhabits Anne Hathaway's cottage, who
is herself a descendent of the Hathaway family; also upon the parish

clerk who conducts the visitor to the chancel of Trinity Church and points out the bust of Shakespeare. . . . All bear witness to the zeal and industry of Mr. Halliwell, under whose auspices so much has been effected to render a visit to Stratford profitable to the Shakespearean student.[10]

The acknowledgement of Halliwell was fitting, for although he had no part in the Stratford ceremonies, the town was much beholden to him. Halliday was rather less impressed, apparently suspecting every native of unbridled rapacity. He parted, reluctantly, with his sixpence at the Birthplace and was distracted from his criticism of the unsympathetic restoration of the property by the sight of two huge Warwickshire policemen in full uniform. The policing of the festival, in fact, cost the Committee £118 10s. Far from finding their presence reassuring Halliday's musings were disrupted by the police-presence, and he parted with yet another sixpence to see the Shakespeare Museum comprising "much mulberry and many clay pipes of modern aspect".

At last even Halliday's resistance crumbled when he took an evening walk to Anne Hathaway's cottage: "That long-expected thrill comes unbidden now. Truly a place to nurse a poet. . . . I find the cottage more real than the house; no paint and varnish here".[11] His guide was the famous Hathaway descendent, Mrs. Mary Baker (née Taylor), who claimed to be Anne Hathaway's great-great-great-niece and who was still alive, aged 80, when the property was finally acquired by the Birthplace Trust from Alderman Thompson in 1892 at a cost of £3,000. Halliday at least was convinced of her legitimacy as she dispensed her authenticating guidance from Shakespeare's courting seat to the black oak bedstead.

Of the distractions arranged especially for the Tercentenary, the Picture Exhibition, which had been suggested by a Mr. E T Craig, a phrenologist from Warwick, was open daily in the reconstructed Town Hall. Arranged by Mr. Hogarth of the Haymarket, the exhibition cost £352 10s. 6d. and even with admission set at 2s. 6d. it was bound to lose money. The coup of the exhibition was the loan from Queen Victoria of the Lawrence portrait of Kemble as Hamlet. It was then unusual for the Queen to loan pictures, and this was the disconsolate Sovereign's only gesture to the Tercentenary, apart from donating the oak for Primrose Hill, and the letter from Sir Charles Beaumont Phipps, Keeper of the Privy Purse to Flower was proudly publicised:

I have had the honour to lay before Her Majesty the Queen the purport of your letter of the 7th instant. The Queen has been obliged for some time past to decline to accede to the numerous applications made to Her Majesty for the loan of pictures from the Royal Galleries for the purpose of public exhibitions. . . .

The Queen has however been graciously pleased to consider this very remarkable occasion as one in favour of which an exception may be made. . . .[12]

The Exhibition mustered no less than twenty-eight portraits of Shakespeare, including one loaned by Lord Leigh. The Earl of Carlisle loaned two Zoffanys of Garrick in *The Mayor of Garratt* and *The Alchemist*. Theodore Martin, less possessive of his pictures than his wife, allowed pictures of Betterton, Woffington, Abington (by Kneller), Garrick (by Reynolds and Gwyn) to be shown. It was an impressive collection, though whether the number of informed viewers justified such a large outlay must be doubtful.

The influence of Garrick's Jubilee was such that the opening events in the Pavilion were both musical. Hunter countered the objection to the performance of *The Messiah* by reference to Garrick and because of the "literary admirers of Shakespeare . . . who, from various reasons would not choose to attend theatrical performances".[13] The principal soloists were Madame Parepa, Messrs. Sims Reeves, George Perren, Patey and Santley, with Miss Baxter substituting for Madame Sainton-Dolby. The band and choirs amounted to over 500, including contingents from the Festival Choral Society, the Amateur Harmonic Society, Birmingham; the Sacred Harmonic Society, London; the Festival Choral Society, Worcester; and Holy Trinity Church Choir, Stratford-upon-Avon. Alfred Mellon presided.

Sims Reeves confounded the sceptics by actually appearing, though his short, dark-haired, figure showed "some occasional traces of recent indisposition".[14] Madame Parepa, who was "in good voice, and indeed in some of her airs, exhibited unwonted force",[15] testified to the superb acoustics of the building. Her delivery of "I know that my Redeemer liveth" was particularly fine.

The Messiah was at noon, and at 7 pm that day The Grand Miscellaneous Concert of Music Associated with the Words of Shakespeare took place. The soloists were mainly the same, Mellon thereby capitalising on their presence in Stratford. There was an orchestra of 120, including Sarah Flower's old music teacher Mr. Griesbach, a violinist. The programme embraced Beethoven's overture *Coriolanus*, settings by Verdi, Arne, Schubert and Mellon himself, in particular his warmly received Shakespearean Overture with Airs, "Soft-Flowing Avon", "Sweet Willie, Oh!" and "Ye Warwickshire Lads and Ye Lasses".

Admission for *The Messiah* was 21s. for Area (stalls) seats, 10s. 6d. for the gallery and 5s. for unreserved seats; corresponding prices for the evening concert were: 10s. 6d., 5s., and 2s. 6d., which, with the less restrictive time, attracted a much larger audience. The festival's policy amounted to audience segregation by pricing. The price virtually determined the social composition of the audience and was indeed a means of keeping away undesirable elements, however earnestly they may have wished to attend. A proportion of cheaper seats at the main events would undoubtedly have resulted in larger attendance, but that came in the second week of popular entertainments. The concert did not end until 11 pm so that there was no question of short-changing at the cheaper rates.

April 26

Carriages left Bridge Street at 1 pm to visit Charlecote, the scene of Shakespeare's legendary deer poaching. The weather continued fine as it did for the whole week. Visitors were enchanted by the beautiful house, its many treasures, the church and the unusual fencing around the park, constructed without a nail as it had been in the twelfth century.

In the evening *Twelfth Night*, presented by the Theatre Royal, Haymarket company, with the Earl of Carlisle, Lord Leigh, Lord Shaftesbury and Sir Robert Hamilton setting the pace for enjoyment in the front row. The Haymarket, of which J B Buckstone had been manager since 1853, had been kind to Stratford. Messrs. Wales and O'Connor had played vital roles in constructing the Pavilion stage and Buckstone himself had dispensed much-needed professional advice. *Twelfth Night* exhibited the talents of his company, and his own as Sir Andrew Aguecheek, to good advantage:

> . . . Then was heard the genial familiar voice of Mr. Buckstone shouting to Sir Toby behind the scenes. Never was heard such applause as was then sent up . . .. The ovation was the heartier perhaps in that it arose as much out of a feeling of satisfaction that Mr. Buckstone, in the midst of defection, had remained true, as out of his great talents as an actor. . . . The great comedian's conception of the character was to our mind perfect . . . he was no mere buffoon, though weak and foolish, no sot though given to drinking.[16]

For the rest: Henry Compton played Feste with admirable quaintness; Rogers was a robust Sir Toby, Farren a mischief-loving Fabian, and Chippendale a thoroughly sustained, rather formal, Malvolio whose cross-gartering was relished by the audience. *Twelfth Night* was followed by E A Sothern in a comedietta, *My Aunt's Advice*.

It was widely broadcast that the evening's performances were being given gratuitously, but Buckstone's generosity knew its bounds and after the festival he wrote to Flower:

> As regards 'Twelfth Night' I had to close the theatre here, but of course paid all my people, just the same as if it had been open, which amounted to £85. On speaking to Mr. Sothern I was surprised to find that he expected £50 for his services – but which he would apply thus – £25 to be paid to him, leaving £25 as a donation to the Stratford fund.[17]

Buckstone also claimed to be £20 out of pocket by releasing three actors to appear in *As You Like It* on 28 April. The Committee sent Buckstone £100, which he received with thanks, protesting that he had hoped that individuals would have played gratuitously. Had Stratford got such good value for every £100 it spent, there would have been nothing to complain of.

April 27

At 2 pm in the Shakespeare Rooms (the 1827 theatre in New Place Gardens) there were Readings from the Works of Shakespeare by Mrs. Macready, interspersed with music from the pianoforte of Mr. Coote. Mrs. Macready was American and no relation of William Charles, though she does not appear to have disabused those who assumed a connection. The audience of around 250 included Howard Staunton who was editing the earliest photographic reproduction of the First Folio and brought along a copy of the first part.

The Wednesday evening was to have been the dramatic climax with Fechter's *Hamlet*, and the programme for the double-bill of *The Comedy of Errors* and *Romeo and Juliet* referred crushingly to his eleventh-hour withdrawal after repeated pledges. The tributes to George Vining and Stella Colas were fulsome and Andrew Halliday commended all concerned: "As an example, the whole of the scenery and properties that were used in Romeo and Juliet at the Princess's Theatre, on Tuesday night, in London, were used in Stratford on Wednesday, and were seen again in London on the evening of Thursday".[18] In order to facilitate scene-changing the shortened version of *The Comedy of Errors* with the Brothers Webb as the Dromios was played first.

The reception for Stella Colas and George Vining (Mercutio) was rapturous, but whereas Buckstone's loyalty was matched by his acting, such was not the case with Mlle Colas. With customary candour Sarah Flower wrote of the actress's beauty, but continued "I could not understand a word",[19] and it is apparent that even the sympathetic Stratfordians succumbed to laughter: "On her entrance the young heroine was much applauded. On her exit everybody was convulsed with suppressed tittering though making formal complimentary noises with their hands".[20] Her Romeo – J Nelson – was inadequate and only Vining and Mrs. Henry Marston, as the Nurse, redeemed the acting honours. Furthermore, the text used was unauthentic, retaining the non-Shakespearean episode in the last act in which the lovers converse with each other. In Stratford a good house of over 3,000 people, was not unduly worried by these inadequacies, but when the performance was repeated in London it attracted widespread opprobrium.

April 28

The Shakespeare Rooms were again used for a small-scale offering – A Concert of Instrumental Music and Glees from Shakespeare's Plays – at 2 pm. In the evening the final play, *As You Like It,* took place in the Pavilion. The cast had been especially assembled with great difficulty. William Creswick was, in modern parlance, director, S May loaned the costumes free, and O'Connor was responsible for the scenery. Compton (Touchstone), Chippendale (Adam) and Farren (Orlando) had stayed on from *Twelfth Night*, which had prepared them for getting the most out of almost continuous carousing at the Washington Irving hotel, The Red Horse; Irving's poker was proudly displayed by the Mayor and Vicar who were frequently to be found there. The local actor James Bennett, at last got his chance as the exiled Duke, a role with which he may have felt some affinity. As Rosalind Mrs. Vezin was inevitably rated as vastly superior to the traitorous Helen Faucit: "A rich banquet of true Shakespearean force. . . . Her elocution was perfect, her action exquisitely true to nature and her appearance charmingly graceful".[21] However, even the London press, venturing that visitors might have caught a glimpse of Touchstone and Audrey in the forest of Arden that week, was enchanted:

> The completeness with which this delightful pastoral play was placed on the stage of the Stratford Pavilion would have satisfied the most critical demands of a London audience. The scenic illusion was preserved throughout by the admirable acting. Mrs. Hermann Vezin, who gained her histrionic reputation as Mrs. Charles Young, played Rosalind with an archness and intelligence that quickly won the hearts of the spectators.[22]

The audience, again over 3,000, must have felt particularly gratified that this production, assembled especially for Stratford, of the play most closely associated with Warwickshire, was such a striking success.

April 29
The finale of the festival proper was "A GRAND FANCY DRESS BALL. . . . To which no one will be admitted except in Fancy Dress, Court Dress or Uniform. . . . No Masks, Dominos, or Pantomime characters will be admitted. Coote and Tinney's Band has been engaged".[23] Something of the flavour of the occasion is gained from the tiny specially-printed pink dance cards; the photographs of Charles and Sarah Flower and their friends posing rather bashfully in full costume in the hall of their home before departing for the ball; and Sarah's diary entry. She engaged a hairdresser from Douglas in Bond Street to dress the high, powdered hair styles which she and her friends were wearing. Male guests had to change and sleep in the brewery offices. They had a gay dinner at 7.30 pm and left for the ball at 10 pm; there she particularly enjoyed dancing with the indefatigable Alfred Mellon "the Quadrilles he had composed for the occasion", and with William Creswick who, dressed as Benedick, had quite a lot to live up to. The ball went on into the not so early hours: "Came home a little before five walking home by broad daylight – the birds singing and the apple trees in full blossom".[24] By then the powdered hair looked a bit grey, but it must have been a night to cherish in the memory, even for the spectators who crowded the galleries at 5s. each, and the Lord Lieutenant and the Mayor, who went dressed as the Lord Lieutenant and the Mayor respectively.

For all the difficulties attending its preparation, the festival week went off without a hitch and was enjoyed by all, save perhaps Mrs. Edward Flower, who said she would rather pay £1,000 than go through it all again. There was some criticism that the gentry, for whom the events were primarily designed, did not patronise them as much as expected, but this complaint seems to have come from the tradespeople who had expected more general business from visitors. The banquet and the ball had attracted virtually capacity attendances; the musical offerings had not been so popular but *The Messiah* had been awkwardly timed for all except the leisured; significantly, the plays had proved most popular and the three performances were undoubtedly the most elaborate and accomplished that the dramatist's birthplace had ever witnessed. The further success of the plays in the following "popular" week encouraged Edward Flower's son Charles in the Memorial Theatre enterprise of the next decade.

Stratford had proved triumphantly that it could do justice to its famous son, and the paltry programme of the London Committee, which had been so condescending to Stratford, amply underlined this. As if to express their approval, the heavens, which had lowered so grievously upon Garrick's Jubilee, shone upon, or at least refrained from drenching, the Tercentenary. The difference was that the Jubilee had been conceived and executed by a Metropolitan actor; the Tercentenary was the creation of Stratfordians themselves. Some measure of the goodwill generated was shown in numerous thankyou letters from performers and in the following advertisement in *The Era*:

> To the Stratford Tercentenary Committee. We the undersigned, members of the Royal Princess's Theatre, London including operatives and every individual on and off the stage, concerned with the representation of *Romeo and Juliet* and *The Comedy of Errors* at Stratford on Wednesday 27 April 1864, beg hereby to return our sincere and grateful thanks for the handsome and liberal manner in which they were entertained and to testify our admiration of the excellence of all the arrangements on that occasion.[25]

POPULAR ENTERTAINMENTS

The Stratford Committee, whose original intention had been to hold a day of "popular entertainment" during the festival, later favoured a separate week instead, for, as Hunter put it: "they apprehended a Boxing Night crush must take place in every street in Stratford if any strong attraction were held out to the million on the first week of the celebration".[26] The social segregation of the first week had not been absolute, and on cattle market day, which coincided with *The Messiah*, the wives and daughters of the more opulent farmers had found their way into the Pavilion. But "The old Warwickshire peasant, in smock-frock and gaiters, with that wonderfully coloured and marvellously twisted red handkerchief about his neck . . . is looking forward wistfully to the Shakespearean equestrian pageant".[27]

The pressure for the Pageant had mounted during April with a boldly printed handbill appearing on the Ides, headed:

TIME! SHAKESPEARE THE POET OF THE PEOPLE
People of Stratford! Where are the seats reserved for you at the

forthcoming festival? What part or lot have you who originated it, in the coming celebration? None! But you will be permitted to see the Fireworks, because they cannot be let off in the Pavilion; and you are promised something for yourself *after the swells have dined*. Only wait till the next week, and see the dainty mess that shall be BREWED for you out of the cold "wittles". PEOPLE OF STRATFORD, who would not see your town disgraced on such an occasion, your streets empty, or blocked up only by the carriages of *profitless swells,* take counsel without delay!
Call a meeting without delay!
Form your own Committee!!
Hold your own Festival!!!
Look to your own business. Lay out your own money.
Get up your own out-door sports and in-door pastimes, and let your watchword be

SHAKESPEARE the POET OF THE PEOPLE
AND HURRAH FOR THE PAGEANT

Hobbesley Hall
Kendal Green
Flowery Land

Ides of April 1864[28]

Clearly there were some in Stratford who were not "cheerfully working in their own appointed sphere", as Archbishop Trench had advocated. The Committee remained adamant about the pageant. Although it was referred to briefly in the official programme, it was arranged by a separate committee, headed by John Talbot, which paid £5 to the corporation for the privilege of proceeding through the streets. Money was raised by a door-to-door canvass of the town which produced more than enough – a measure of the popularity of the pageant.

The pageant's popularity was not limited to the citizens of Stratford, and an estimated 30,000 people thronged the town on Monday 2 May. Cheap trains were run from Gloucester, Bristol, Worcester, Birmingham, Rugby and the north; omnibuses crowded in from Coventry and vehicles converged from every direction. Such was its success that the pageant was repeated on the following day, when any minor blemishes were corrected.

The pageant was no homespun affair for it was the fortunate beneficiary of the generosity of Jean Frederick Ginnett, the circus proprietor, who placed his stud of horses and equestrian performers at the disposal of the committee free of charge. Dresses, armour and other accoutrements were supplied by J Nathan and Winter of Leicester Square, London and the whole was marshalled by Joseph Tyrrell, the Liverpool stage-manager. The procession included heralds and banners, Melpomene and Thalia (as in 1830), and most of the principal characters from the plays. It proceeded through the town, pausing for the performance of "solemn and appropriate Shakespearean music by Dr. Arne"[29] outside the Birthplace.

The 1830 pageant may have been regarded as a "Brummagem affair" by the gentry, whose opinion of that in 1864 would probably have been the same. However, it demonstrated that Stratford was capable of attracting a mass public, one which was far more advantageous to local trade than the gentry who attended the first week. Various popular entertainments including Wombwell's Menagerie added to the delights of the second week.

The second week's official programme was of a more restrained nature ("dainty mess"), but it was well patronised by those who might have resented their virtual exclusion from the first week. On Saturday 30 April a Grand Promenade Concert took place in the Pavilion at 2 pm, admission 1s. The programme included Mendelssohn, Gounod, Verdi and Meyerbeer. On Monday 2nd, Coxwell's Grand Balloon failed to ascend at 2 pm, but the Band of the Scots Greys was at hand to render a varied programme. In the evening "an Efficient Quadrille Band" was engaged for the Public Ball in the Pavilion, admission 2s. 6d., with refreshments at "moderate charges" from the ever-resourceful Mr. Mountford of Worcester.

The Shakespearean offerings consisted of *Othello* on 3 May and *Much Ado About Nothing*, with the Trial Scene from *The Merchant of Venice*, on 4 May, both prepared by Creswick with admission set at 3s, 2s and 1s. Excursion trains were at hand to convey audiences home to Wolverhampton, Worcester, Warwick, etc., after the performances.

For *Othello* Creswick played the title part, with the local James Bennett coming into his own as Iago:

> The excellence and esprit of the performance was not confined to the chief parts, and they were all played well before a house of 4,000 persons. The little town, indeed, has never been so full before as it was that night.[30]

Amongst the crowded audience were the butler and coachmen of the Revd. Julian Charles Young of Ilmington, who had sent his servants to the play in recognition of their labours in looking after his guests in the previous week:

> I then went to the stables and asked my coachman, an honest, simple creature, but not over-burdened with imagination, how he had been impressed with what he had seen. Grinning from ear to ear with pleasurable reminiscences, he replied with infinitely more alacrity than his predecessor [the butler] – ' 'Twas really beautiful, Sir. I liked it unaccountable!' The cheerful face clouded over as I asked him what it was about. 'I don't ezactly know, Sir!' . . . 'Oh! I know, Sir, now; I know. It ran upon sweethearting! Aye that it did. And there were two gennelmen, one was in white, and the other was in black; and, what was more, both o' these gents was sweet on the same gal.'.[31]

The next night Mrs. Vezin, the triumphant Rosalind of the previous week, played Beatrice to Creswick's Benedick, with her husband as Claudio and Bennett as Don Pedro. The Vezins dined with the Charles

Flowers before the performance and Mrs. Vezin felt too poorly to act. Happily a Doctor Ebbage was at hand; he nursed her through the evening and her stage-fright was not apparent to the audience: "Mrs. Hermann Vezin and Mr. Creswick deservedly brought down the house and received repeated applause. She spoke with the utmost ease, and every syllable went straight to the ear".[32] The Trial, with Bennett as Shylock and Mrs. Vezin as Portia, was something of an anti-climax, but the great festival was not to end on such a note. Three cheers were called for the Mayor and were succeeded by three for the Vicar; whilst the roof was still echoing a further solitary cheer rang out. There was no need to ask for whom that was.

The London Programme

With the artistic wealth of the capital around it the National Shakespeare Committee aspired to a grand programme. In February *The Athenaeum* announced that the lessees of Drury Lane, Covent Garden, the Haymarket, the Princess's, the Adelphi and Lyceum had promised performances in aid of the fund and that the Surrey and Strand were likely to follow suit. Circulars had been sent to forty-three provincial theatres inviting co-operation and assistance. The musical profession was equally forthcoming, with *The Messiah* planned for 23 April and a grand concert at Exeter Hall with Mr. and Mrs. German Reed.

In due course the National Shakespeare Committee advertised its Official Programme, boasting over thirty Musical Artistes and nearly one hundred Dramatic Artistes appearing at most of the theatres mentioned in the February bulletin. However, this did not disguise the fact that the National Shakespeare Committee itself had produced virtually nothing and was simply collecting together various performances which individual theatres would have mounted anyway. Its efforts and the limitations of those performances were summarised devastatingly:

> The Metropolitan commemoration of the Tercentenary of Shakespeare under the auspices of the Committee has been limited to a few dramatic performances at various theatres, and these have been for the most part marred by the blemishes which appear to attach inevitably to everything that is touched on by that ill-starred body. Thus for example, at one house we had "The Taming of the Shrew" without that induction that was the poet's first comic masterpiece; at another "The 1st Part of King Henry IV" with the scene between Falstaff and Hal expunged; at a third "Romeo and Juliet" in Garrick's garbled version . . .; at a fourth "The Merchant of Venice" with the omission of that last act wanting which the idea of the drama . . . remains but partially developed. . . . But after all the National Shakespeare Committee did nothing more than nod its head when these several programmes were submitted to it – and considering its condition of general dormancy, it may be charitably supposed that the several managers mistook the nod of drowsiness for a nod of approval.[1]

Deserving no credit for these offerings, the National Committee could hardly be held responsible for their shortcomings. Nevertheless they constitute an interesting range of Shakespearean productions of the period. Many were not new – *Twelfth Night* at the Haymarket and *The Merchant of Venice* at Sadler's Wells for instance – but three deserve some consideration: *Henry IV i* at Drury Lane, *Romeo and Juliet* at the Princess's and *Henry VI ii* at the Surrey.

After his misfortunes with Fechter at the Lyceum, Phelps had settled down as the leading actor at Drury Lane, under the management of Edmund Falconer and F R Chatterton where, for *Henry IV i*, he was surrounded by many of the most considerable acting talents of the day: Ryder (Henry IV), Vandenhoff (Mortimer) and Rose Leclercq (Lady Percy). Prices ranged from 6s. stalls to 6d. upper gallery.

For the Birthday performance, *Henry IV i* was preceded by the "ring scene" from *Twelfth Night* and followed by a poetical masque entitled "The Fairies' Festival in Commemoration of Shakespeare's Birthday" written by Falconer:

A deputation, consisting of a poet, an actor, an editor, and a critic, is introduced by Puck, who explains that it is proposed to celebrate the three hundredth birthday of Shakespeare. The royal pair (Oberon and Titania) willingly promise to patronise the festival. There were in this scene some very feeling and graceful allusions to the sorrow which has clouded our Queen, which were well received by the audience. The festival takes place in a sylvan retreat in Windsor Forest.[2]

Of the substantive piece Henry Morley has left a detailed account. The omission of the "Crown and cushion" scene between Falstaff and Hal was explained by the actor's emphasis upon "the lively intellect that stands for soul as well as mind in his gross body," as a result of which "the fat knight, who so familiarly cracks his jokes with the Prince or upon Bardolph, is not vulgarised in Mr. Phelps's reading".[3] By way of compensation "the Glendower scene and Welsh song were restored". The performance indicates the extent to which actors were still pruning the texts to accommodate their own and their audiences' susceptibilities.

The preference for Garrick's version of *Romeo and Juliet* at the Princess's was another example. Stella Colas still had her supporters: "We could discover no drawback in the performance, mentally and physically Mdlle Colas is Juliet";[4] but Morley considered: "There was nothing like the frantic enthusiasm of the first reception. . . . The Lady has returned to us not quite so bad as she was; and the public applauds her not quite so much as it did".[5] This time Morley managed to watch the performance through as he had been unable to previously, but found himself exasperated by Colas's mispronunciations and dependence on distracting and unnecessary movements: "[she] jerks her head, grins, twists, ambles from one side of the stage to the other, and looks obtrusively conscious of every part of herself from the tip of her nose to the tips of her shoes".[6] At least the critics were at one in dismissing John Nelson's Romeo as beneath contempt, though admirers of Mlle Colas tended to resent his lack of fire and animation more.

The discerning Morley, sometime Professor of English Literature at University College, London, realised the gulf between critical and popular acclaim, and yet he did not record the most enterprising production of the Tercentenary – James Anderson's *Henry VI ii* at the Surrey. Anderson's short-lived management at the Surrey was a brave attempt at bringing a repertoire of quality to a transpontine theatre, and he considered "the tercentenary of Shakespeare's birthday . . . an excellent opportunity to produce his historical play of *Henry VI*".[7] Nothing daunted by the fifty speaking parts his small company doubled, trebled and even quadrupled, being "mightily pleased with their parts". Anderson himself played York, appropriating Warwick's powerful accusation of Suffolk: "This accusation gave Mr. Anderson the opportunity of exhibiting to their full extent the dramatic powers of which he is possessed".[8] Anderson also played Jack Cade to less unanimous praise.

The "piece has been most liberally produced as far as costumes, armour, scenery, and adjuncts are concerned",[9] but as Anderson complained: "The play achieved an immense success but drew no money; I got only twelve nights out of it"[10] and a critic who returned on Tuesday 28 April observed a thin and listless assembly, which discredited "the intellectual inhabitants of Southwark and Lambeth".[11] Thus even when rarities were done with distinction and critically acclaimed, audiences were still slow to respond.

In music the National Committee could not rely upon a suitable existing concert programme and advertised three events: a programme of songs and readings at St. James's Hall on 22 April; a Festival Concert and Dramatic Readings at the Royal Agricultural Hall on 21 April; and a further programme there on 23 April. The extent of the National Shakespeare Committee's responsibility for these occasions was uncertain; for instance, a critic observed of the St. James's Hall concert: "Whether the concert in question was destined in any way to benefit the various funds now being raised with reference to the Tercentenary Festival was not stated on the programme".[12]

Nevertheless, the St. James's Hall concert on 22 April did not escape the usual Tercentenary vicissitudes: "The artistes from Her Majesty's Theatre did not appear in the order announced", but "they did appear, and that was the point".[13] Then the ubiquitous Mrs. Macready, who was scheduled to give two Dramatic Recitals (*The Merchant of Venice* 4.1 and *A Midsummer Night's Dream* 2.2) gave only the former. The organisational disorder did not ruin the evening: Fanny Huddart's "She never told her love" (Arne) and Mr. Santley's "Under the Greenwood Tree" (Arne) particularly delighted the audience and "the participation of Mdlle Titiens, Signor Giuglini, and M. Gassier in a concert in honour of Our National Poet's memory, may be taken as a graceful tribute on their part".[14]

Both the concerts at the Royal Agricultural Hall, and a Character Ball and Masque, held there on 9 April at which "the Colossal TERCEN-TENARY BUST" modelled by Charles Bacon was unveiled, were advertised as being "Under the direction of the National Shakespeare Committee". For these occasions the cavernous hall had been decorated with pink drapery, masking the spaces beneath the gallery, and inn signs, including Ye Tabard and The Boar's Head, hung along the sides.

The programme for Thursday 21 consisted of songs from Shakespeare and readings. Performers included Fanny Huddart, this time with "Under the Greenwood Tree"; Mme Parepa; Mme Sainton-Dolby; Mme Lem-mens-Sherrington; and Sims Reeves with "Sigh no more ladies" and "Blow, blow, thou wintry wind". The chorus delivered "England's Minstrel King", "the words by Linnaeus Banks Esq., composed expressly for the occasion" and the indefatigable Samuel Phelps recited the entire first act of *The Tempest*. Although the artists were the same as, or of equal calibre to, those performing at Stratford, the Agricultural Hall was geared towards a more socially-diverse audience with "Prices of Admission: – Stall Chairs, 5s; Reserved Seats, 3s; Galleries, 2s; Area, 1s. A few Cushioned Chairs, in best position, 10s. 6d.".[15]

If the tenor of the 21 April concert was musically and socially catholic, that of the 23 April programme was decidedly egalitarian, for it was advertised as "Grand Miscellaneous Entertainment and Monster Demon-stration of the Working Classes" with admission at 1s. This was the fruit of the overture made by the National Shakespeare Committee, in the person of G Linnaeus Banks, to the Working Men's Shakespeare Committee. The programme again included Miss Huddart and Mme. Parepa, with a strong dramatic contribution from J L Toole, Stratford's stalwart James Bennett; and Henry Marston, reciting Eliza Cook's special ode. In spite of these attractions and "Band and Chorus of 2,000", all for 1s., the Committee reported "that in consequence of the comparatively small support given to this Festival, owing to a conflicting enthusiasm which prevailed at the moment, a very serious deficiency arose. . . ."[16] In fact the Working Men's Committee's share of receipts came to only £10.

The "conflicting enthusiasm" was the planting, by Samuel Phelps, of the oak sapling, given by the Queen, on Primrose Hill earlier that day. What at first sight may have seemed a quintessentially English ceremony had become, by 23 April, the pretext for a political protest which had nothing to do with celebrating Shakespeare.

Garibaldi's visit to England in the Spring of 1864 had prompted "a more triumphant welcome than any other visitor to England had ever received".[17] He was feted everywhere – Parliament, Eton College and the Crystal Palace – and by all ranks including the Prince of Wales; but when it seemed that Garibaldi was going to extend his visit indefinitely, the government became apprehensive. In an inept interview Gladstone, the Chancellor of the Exchequer, intimated this concern to the visitor who decided to leave. Speculation about the reason for Garibaldi's departure was rife and not satisfied by the official explanation of ill-health, so that when he left England aboard the Duke of Sutherland's yacht *Undine* on the morning of Saturday 23 April there was a disaffected element poised to exploit the situation.

This they were well placed to do, for "A large proportion of the members of the Garibaldi Committee (a special Working Men's Committee) are also members of the Shakespeare Committee, which was the principal reason why Primrose Hill was selected for the Garibaldi meeting".[18] In addition to its attractions as an elevated open space 207 feet above the Thames, Primrose Hill had others of a more sociological nature, for it joined, or separated, working-class Chalk Farm and the genteel fringe of Regent's Park, so that an event held there would attract the support of the former and the attention of the latter: "The working classes are invited to attend in thousands and we regret to observe that their presence is to be taken advantage of in order to set up a Garibaldi demonstration in opposition to the departure, as this is mixing up two distinct matters".[19]

The ceremony was slow to get underway. A procession from Russell Square led by George Cruikshank, the illustrator, at the head of the Havelock Volunteers of which he was Colonel, was late and mustered short of 500; but already assembled on the hill was a crowd variously estimated at 15–20,000 (in the press) and 70–100,000 (by the Working Men's Committee). The location for the tree was "at the foot of the hill on its south-eastern side facing Ormunde Terrace"[20] There guests and more affluent onlookers were positioned in a small enclosure in which "had been erected a small platform covered with some of the serge used in the late Garibaldi demonstration".[21]

Richard Moore, of the Working Men's Shakespeare Committee, introduced Samuel Phelps, who proclaimed: "The sight around me is one of the noblest and one of the grandest spectacles that ever met the human eye. In the name of the workmen of England I plant this oak and trust that it may live and flourish and reach maturity".[22] Mrs. Linnaeus Banks then christened the tree with Avon water and Henry Marston recited the specially composed ode by Eliza Cook, whose *New Echoes and Other Poems* appeared in the Tercentenary year.

At the end of the ceremony a splinter group of 60–70 gathered at the top of the hill and encouraged the crowds to regroup around them, of which about 4,000 did so. The principal speaker was Edmond Beales, Etonian, Cambridge graduate, then Recording Magistrate for Middlesex and subsequently a County Court Circuit judge, but first and foremost a political agitator, who was President of the Reform League at the time of the Hyde Park riots in July 1866. Beales asserted that "the main and true facts connected with the departure of the General had been suppressed"[23] and alleged a conspiracy between Palmerston and Louis Napoleon. At this point an officer from S division, supported by a strong body of police, made his way to the centre of the meeting and informed the chairman that "his orders were not to allow any political meeting to take place on Primrose Hill".[24]

Although the crowd seemed to be motivated more by curiosity than agitation, the intervention of the police, who were clearly very nervous, promoted considerable resentment and only Mr. Hartwell's appeal for quiet and Mr. Cremer's adjournment of the meeting prevented physical violence. The dissident leaders adjourned to the Adelaide Arms in Chalk Farm, where, with Mr. Wiseass in the chair, they unanimously adopted a resolution protesting "in the strongest manner possible against the forcible suppression by the police of the Garibaldi meeting on Primrose Hill, as an unjustifiable interference with the liberties of the people".[25] They appointed a deputation to wait upon the Home Secretary and ascertain whether any special instructions had been issued to the police for the Primrose Hill gathering. Indeed Sir G Gray was asked that question in the House of Commons on Monday 25 April, when he replied that the police action was part of the general policy against "meetings and assemblies of persons for the making of speeches and discussing exciting and popular topics which might lead to disorder . . . in public parks".[26]

The press resounded with protests and accusations from Beales and his confederates for some weeks, but with Garibaldi gone they could not generate any real momentum, though their grievance smouldered on, coming to flash-point in Hyde Park on 23 July 1866.

The Primrose Hill incident was hardly a scheduled part of the programme adumbrated by the National Committee, and elsewhere other more peaceful celebrations escaped its Janus-faced nod. Amongst them was an Actors' Supper at the Freemasons' Hall, Great Queen Street, on the eve of the Birthday at an hour (11.45 pm) to suit those who were performing, and at a price (5s.) to suit those who were not. Andrew Halliday marvelled at Shakespeare's all-embracing attraction: "All classes and degrees mingling on equal terms of brotherhood in honour of the great High Priest of their art. . . . Up they went, a strangely amalgamated crowd of leading tragedians and comedians, rubbing shoulders with general utility, and supernumeraries, and pantomimists, and prompters, and call-boys, and even door-keepers".[27] Banner-carriers outnumbered Macbeths by a hundred to one, but alike, at the beginning, they applauded the unveiling of a statue of the Bard.

Ben Webster was in the chair and J B Buckstone was Vice-Chairman. Seven toasts were drunk, and, amongst the speakers, Buckstone succumbed to the unstinting lyricism which the Tercentenary evoked especially in actors: "This day 300 years ago a baby boy was born in the low-roofed room at Stratford-upon-Avon. . . . The happy mother of that boy, while listening to his "mewling and pining", never dreamt of the immortality awaiting the little stranger nestling at her bosom".[28]

The highlight of the evening was a sonnet written for the occasion by the Irish-born actor and writer John Brougham, set to music by Alfred Mellon. Its performance was greeted by cries for the author and composer; the Chairman explained that Mellon was unavoidably absent (no doubt preoccupied with arrangements for Stratford), but Brougham responded, referring to Mellon "who had so magnificently embalmed his (Brougham's) poor fly in the amber of his music".[29]

The Crystal Palace at Sydenham, which had so recently welcomed Garibaldi, prepared its own Shakespearean offering. Although the Primrose Hill gathering provided a convenient alibi for disappointing attendance, several thousands were present at the open-air concert. Soloists included Mme. Parepa and W H Cummings, but the most gripping moment was the emergence of Shakespeare himself from a replica of his birthplace. Alas, he was no more genuine than the house, but an actor, Arthur Young, was dressed and made-up to resemble Shakespeare. He followed this *coup de théâtre* with a solo-rendering of the incantation scene from *Macbeth*.

A less dramatic, but possibly more authentic, representation of Shakespeare was on view at the National Portrait Gallery, where the Chandos portrait was on display, about which George Scharf junior had penned *A Few Observations Connected with the Chandos Portrait of Shakespeare Presented to the National Portrait Gallery by the Earl of Ellesmere.*

No citizen of London could complain that he lacked the opportunity to observe the Tercentenary in an appropriate way; whether on Primrose Hill, at the Crystal Palace, or at one of the principal Metropolitan theatres. However, the National Shakespeare Committee failed signally in its attempt at galvanising the nation's capital to a wholehearted celebration of the event.

The Legacy

The legacy which both the London and Stratford committees wished to leave was a memorial to Shakespeare in the form of a statue and both failed to achieve this.

The National Shakespeare Committee established a sub-committee headed by the Duke of Manchester and including Sir Joseph Paxton, Thomas Donaldson (Joint President of the Institution of British Architects), two MPs, William Cowper (Commissioner of Works) and William Tite, the painter Daniel Maclise, and A J B Beresford. They deliberated over styles (Classical, Gothic or Tudor) and sites (South Kensington, Green Park or the Embankment), but all to no avail.

Dixon's high hopes had not been realised and in a statement of 20 June 1864 the committee announced:

> The subscription list now amounts to 2500l; expenditure to about 970l; balance about 1280l. The balance, it is thought, may be somewhat increased not so largely as to justify . . . a costly scheme for a memorial . . . but . . . a monument of Shakespeare at least equal in importance to the statues which foreign countries have erected to their national poets . . . may be secured.[1]

In the circumstances the Executive Committee counselled that "the above balance . . . be invested, with a view to its increase, until the Thames Embankment shall have been built".

The National Committee's constituent parts fragmented after the Tercentenary. On 11 May Dickens chaired a meeting of the Royal Dramatic College at the Theatre Royal, Adelphi and observed, to general acclaim: "First of all I will take leave to remark that we do not come here in commemoration of Shakespeare".[2] The Working Men's Shakespeare Committee was more persistent and issued an address appealing for "a statue, ten or twelve feet in height" with "an ornamental shrine of iron and glass to enclose it"[3] for an estimated cost of £3000, but Dickens's response that "Shakespeare's best monument is his works"[4] characterised the lack of enthusiasm for the project.

The National Shakespeare Committee's balance continued to attract controversy and suggestions. In 1864 C L Gruneisen, music critic and Secretary of the Conservative Land Society, who had been active in both Stratford and London, had responded publicly to the Committee's report with this proposal: "I beg respectfully to suggest that it would be far better to appropriate the funds in hand, after audit of expenditure, to the Dramatic College for the schools".[5] He was to return to this suggestion some years later.

In 1867 an ardent French Shakespearean, the Chevalier de Chatelain, demanded: "Nous voulons savoir ce qu'on a fait, ce qu'on fera des £1,280 restées au crédit du monument de Shakespeare".[6]

Gruneisen and the Chevalier were amongst those present at a meeting of National Shakespeare Committee subscribers held in July 1871. There it was revealed, as many must have suspected, that the figures given in 1864 bore little relation to actual cash in hand: "It was true that subscriptions reached, in round numbers, over £2,200, but of this sum only about £1,260 had been received, and the outlay had reached over £970 leaving a balance in hand of about £280".[7] Thus, like so much to do with the National Shakespeare Committee, the balance of £1,280 adumbrated in 1864 owed more to wishful thinking than to reality. Some disquiet was expressed at the manner in which the expenditure of £970 had been spent, in particular the payment of £144 15s. 6d. and £112 3s. 7d. to G Linnaeus Banks and J S Coyne respectively, whose roles as Honorary Dramatic Secretaries had been abandoned for less honorific, but more remunerative, functions.

Nevertheless the National Shakespeare Committee still had a balance the smallness of which did not inhibit the range of suggestions proferred. The statue lobby was still vociferous though opposed by Gruneisen, who again pressed the case of the Royal Dramatic College, but to no avail. Although the College survived until nearly the end of the decade, it was already apparent that its fortunes were on the decline and the National Shakespeare Committee probably sensed that it would be backing another loser. Not that this forestalled the Committee's undiminished instinct for pursuing the impractical. Hepworth Dixon proposed that they should "endeavour to get in the outstanding subscriptions for the purpose of carrying out the original object for which the fund was subscribed," and the meeting concluded with the conviction that "there will be no difficulty to reach the £1,200 . . . so that a monument on the Thames Embankment, as near as possible opposite to the site of the Globe Theatre, of Shakespeare may be looked for in due course".[8]

It is not surprising that their naive belief that defaulters of seven years standing would obligingly pay up proved to be ill-founded.

The Chevalier and Gruneisen were nothing if not tenacious. In 1873 the subject was raised again, initiated by a letter to *The Era* signed Germanicus, imputing the dereliction of national duty in failing to erect "a characteristic ornamental railing and tablet" around the Primrose Hill oak which was "still enclosed by the temporary and trumpery wooden pailing with which it was hastily fenced in nine years ago".[9] G Linnaeus Banks, mindful perhaps of his remuneration, replied that "A Committee is in course of formation", and he and Walter Joyce of the Charing Cross Theatre issued a new prospectus for "subscriptions from 2/6 upwards . . . [for] a characteristic ornamental iron palisade, adorned by an equally characteristic tablet . . . the estimated cost of which will be about £200".[10]

Such a sum could have been met by the balance of the National Shakespeare Committee as the Chevalier de Chatelain pointed out, erroneously retaining the belief that the balance was £1,280:

> Now from 1864 up to the present day the amount of the balance (£1,280) has produced interest. Why not take the sum destined with the capital to erect a *pretended statue to Shakespeare in the Temple* when the Thames embankment shall be finished – the said unoccupied money for the embellishment of Primrose Hill.[11]

The Chevalier generously enclosed 10s. 6d.

He should have known better, the palisade was never erected. Two years later in 1875 it was Gruneisen's turn to direct attention to the National Committee's nest egg. At a meeting in Mr. Graves's Art Gallery in Pall Mall in connection with a performance of *As You Like It* in aid of the appeal for Stratford's Shakespeare Memorial Theatre, attended by Charles Flower, Gruneisen alluded to the National Shakespeare Committee's surplus saying he thought that, "as this Theatre would be a statue to Shakespeare, the application of the money to building the theatre would be quite within the original intention of the donors".[12] Alas, the tentative rapprochement, like Gruneisen's earlier proposal, came to nothing.

As late as 1894, when he published his memoirs, John Cordy Jeaffreson alluded to "a modest sum of money, which may be serviceable to Shakespearean celebrants in 1964",[13] but the Committee's bankers Coutts and Co. report that they can "find no trace of it".[14] Nevertheless the spirit of the London celebrations was revived in 1964 when the Society for Theatre Research planted a replacement oak (the 1864 oak having disappeared long ago) in the same spot on Primrose Hill.[15]

Ironically, within a decade of the Tercentenary, a benefactor emerged who was only too eager to sponsor a Shakespeare memorial. Albert Grant, maverick MP and art collector, purchased the then dilapidated Leicester Fields in 1873, and commissioned Signor Fontana to reproduce Paul Scheemaker's statue of Shakespeare as the centre-piece of Leicester Square, as it remains to this day.[16]

However, the National Shakespeare Committee could claim a more important if more tenuous achievement. In 1864 the little-heard voice of Effingham William Wilson had suggested a London memorial in the form of a theatre, and in 1904 a Stratford emigré, Richard Badger, raised the idea again well in advance of the death tercentenary in 1916. A meeting took place at the Mansion House on 28 February 1905 with Dr. Furnivall as Chairman and Professor Israel Gollancz as Hon. Secretary of what was designated the Shakespeare Memorial Committee. Its commitment to a Shakespeare Memorial National Theatre was determined in March 1909 when Sir Carl Meyer's donation of £70,000 inaugurated the appeal for that objective.

The war frustrated these plans, but as Geoffrey Whitworth and John Elsom[17] have shown the momentum continued between the wars and achieved a new pitch with the House of Commons debate of 21 January

J O Halliwell, founder of the National Shakespeare Fund

LIVE IT
DOWN.

None but himself can be his parallel.
SHAKSPEARE.

PROPOSED DESIGN FOR THE NATIONAL SHAKSPEARE MEMORIAL.—(SUGGESTED BY TWO WELL-KNOWN MEMBERS OF THE LONDON COMMITTEE.)

A cartoon design for the National Shakespeare Memorial, representing two well-known members of the London Committee: W Hepworth Dixon in the chair and J Cordy Jeaffreson on the plinth

The open-air celebration at the Crystal Palace

The concert at the Agricultural Hall in the presence of the colossal TERCENTENARY BUST

Romeo and Juliet, with John Nelson and Stella Colas, at the Princess's

Henry IV i, with Phelps as Falstaff, at Drury Lane

The Battle of Shrewsbury from *Henry IV i* at Drury Lane

Mrs. Linnaeus Banks christening the Shakespeare Oak with Avon water on Primrose Hill

1949 in which Oliver Lyttleton made his eloquent appeal, evoking Carl Meyer's historic 1909 donation. Fourteen years later the National Theatre was installed at the Old Vic and in 1976 it moved into its own premises on the South Bank.

It can no doubt be argued that had the Tercentenary National Shakespeare Committee never existed, the National Theatre would still have come about, but that does not invalidate the chain of continuity connecting the two.

In Stratford the continuity is more self-evident, being exemplified in the name of the Flower family. It is characteristic of the family's devotion to Shakespeare in Stratford that although Edward Flower disapproved of the statue proposal, he followed it up most diligently. As in London a special sub-committee was formed including Carlisle, Hamilton, three MPs, the most notable being Austen Henry Layard, the hero of the Nineveh excavations, Tom Taylor, Theodore Martin, C L Gruneisen, Tennyson and Ruskin. Six of them took two days looking at possible sites and presented a thorough report on 2 March 1864, recommending the Bridge Street location for:

> the memorial is to combine a building, with a statue of the poet, and . . . its general form is to be a covered Loggia, admitting of decoration in plastic material, and in colour and enclosing a central figure of Shakespeare. . . .[18]

One sculptor, Digby Wyatt, pressed Flower with detailed plans; and Flower's successor as mayor and the main advocate of the memorial, James Cox, later worked on a scheme for a vaulted statue-chamber with Oxford sculptor John Gibbs, to cost £3,620,[19] but, like London, Stratford had to wait for an outside benefactor. In 1887 Henry Irving unveiled "an ingenious architectural marriage of a clock and a fountain in the popular Gothic style"[20] in Rother Market, donated by his friend W G Childs, proprietor of the *Philadelphia Journal*. Only the next year Lord Ronald Gower presented his bronze statues of the seated Shakespeare surrounded by Hamlet, Hal, Falstaff and Lady Macbeth.

As with the National Shakespeare Committee, Stratford's failure to build a memorial was due to lack of money. The Stratford Committee was characteristically punctilious in publishing its accounts, which were prepared for a Special Meeting of the Committee on 24 August 1864. Inevitably they were not a final tally; in the case of the Pavilion, for instance, they could record its final selling value but not its cost, which was still under negotiation. Nevertheless there could be no dodging the fact that the deficit would be around £3,000, and Flower was not one to shirk the implications. He drafted a letter in which he suggested the establishment of a guarantee fund. He realised that the problem would be to carry those committee members whose enthusiasm had waned since the festival and proclaimed: "Someone must begin so here I go with E F Flower – £500 0s. 0d; Charles Flower–£250 0s. 0d; Edgar Flower – £250 0s. 0d.".[21]

Although it was too late for them to achieve anything, it was only natural that post-mortems should be held on what had gone wrong financially. Hunter proffered some rather feeble explanations in his record: "the sum expended in advertising . . .; postage stamps, in one quarter of the year (cost) nearly forty pounds."[22] He considered that another contributory cause had been a flood disaster in Sheffield, which had created great hardship and constituted a rival attraction for any "floating" donations.

The Athenaeum reviewed Hunter's book with characteristic aloofness: "In literary quality it is not below the average of provincial good books", its faults are "excusable in a chronicler of country doings".[23] Predictably, it viewed Stratford's main error as its decision to make the celebrations national in scale.

The Saturday Review gave a more considered analysis: "Of these various performances the sermons and the procession were the best of the show – the sermons because they cost nothing; and the procession because the Committee had nothing to do with it".[24] More seriously it pointed out that the advertising was indeed disproportionate to the revenue it attracted. The proportion of subscriptions unpaid was extremely high; in the monument fund £852 15s. 6d., as compared with £471 11s. 7d. actually paid. Other major factors were the inflated cost of the Pavilion and the expenses of the performers, £1,508 9s. 5d., plus the excessive £747 6s. 5d. for "Refreshments for Performers, Dinner and Ball"; Hamlet's injunction to see "the players well bestowed" had been liberally observed.

In his *The Tercentenary. A Retrospect* the new mayor, James Cox, attacked "the utilitarian spirit which . . . decided that nothing should be done to honour the great bard that had not for its end and object something that should be of benefit to us or our children",[25] claiming that concentration on a statue would have brought results.

On the whole, though, Stratford did not go in for agonising post-mortems, but put its mistakes down to experience and looked with undiminishing pride on its achievements. In 1872 the 1827 theatre, which had hampered Halliwell's work on New Place Gardens, was demolished; it may have been the realisation that Stratford was once again without a theatre that prompted Charles Edward Flower to donate a riverside site for the erection of a theatre and to take the initiative in fund-raising. In 1875 a Shakespeare Memorial Association was founded to attract donations for the building and many Tercentenary names lent their support: Lord Leigh, Sir Robert Hamilton, J B Buckstone, James Cox, Edgar Flower and his sons, E A Sothern and Ben Webster; but by then Edward Flower was living in London. Rather than delay until adequate funds were collected, architects were invited to submit plans for a theatre, to which a library and gallery would be added, and the contract was awarded to Messrs. Dodgshun and Unsworth of Westminster.

On 23 April, with £10,000 in the bank, Lord Leigh laid the foundation stone with full Masonic honours. William Creswick made a rather inept speech and Theodore and Helen Martin (Faucit) looked on. Already the London press was pouring cold water on the scheme:

We beg distinctly and indignantly to protest against the whole paltry and impertinent business. . . . They have no mandate to speak in the name of the public or to invest with the attribute of a national undertaking a little mutual admiration club whose object is to endow Stratford with a spick and span new Elizabethan building . . . to be half theatre and half mechanics institute. . . . The rest of the Governors and Council are respectable nobodies.[26]

After its Tercentenary experiences Stratford could ignore such comments and claim that when it came to Shakespeare memorialising its "nobodies" were infinitely more effective than London's or anywhere else's. The Shakespeare Memorial Theatre opened on 23 April 1879, with a production of *Much Ado About Nothing* by Barry Sullivan in which Helen Faucit at last fulfilled her Stratford engagement, as Beatrice, and it survived until it was destroyed by fire on 6 March 1926. By then its resemblance to Shakespeare's Globe was seen to be slight, and other inadequacies were readily pointed out, though as Ruth Ellis observed, "two of its qualities are not in question. It had intimacy and good acoustics . . . and the shape of the auditorium made the audience a compact and unified whole".[27]

In 1932 the new Memorial Theatre was opened and finally Stratford's efforts on behalf of her most famous son were honoured by a royal visitor, the Prince of Wales, who was welcomed by the descendants of those who had failed to involve his namesake in 1864 – Sir Archibald Flower and Lord Leigh, Lord Lieutenant of Warwickshire. Thenceforward Stratford's fame and fortune have been more and more closely entwined with its theatre, a process which began with the pioneering events of 1864.

The Times leader on the Tercentenary contrasted the efforts of the celebrants unfavourably with the qualities which it attributed to Shakespeare:

We have a hero – one of the least envious, most peaceful, most sympathetic of men, "our sweetest Shakespeare" to remember and our fond committees pay him a tribute of infinite jealousies, of interminable squabbles, and of selfishness curious in its ingenuity.[28]

Of jealousies, squabbles and selfishness there was certainly good measure, but on the credit side Shakespeare had never been celebrated on such a scale before, and much that was done anticipated major commemorative and cultural developments of the century ahead. If the shades of Flower, Carlisle, Bellew, Halliwell, Dixon and company look down from some celestial committee room upon the theatres, galleries, libraries and other institutions which honour Shakespeare today, they may justifiably feel entitled to some credit for them.

Notes

THE BEGINNINGS

1. see: Christian Deelman *The Great Shakespeare Jubilee*, 1964; and Johanne M Stockholm *Garrick's Folly*, 1964.
2. Deelman op. cit. p. 259.
3. Robert Hunter *Shakespeare and Stratford-upon-Avon Together With a Full Report of the Tercentenary Celebration*, 1864, p. 74.
4. Mrs. A Mathews *Memoirs of Charles Mathews Comedian*, 1838, v. 3, p. 168.
5. ibid. pp. 168–9.
6. ibid, p. 204.
7. Lou Warwick *Theatre Unroyal*, 1974, pp. 85–90.
8. *The Times* 15.10.1861.
9. Letter 9.6.1863 to Dr. Kingsley in the J O Halliwell Collection of Letters in the University of Edinburgh Library.
10. Hunter op. cit. p. 88.
11. Letter 29.3.1864 from the Earl of Warwick in Dr. Kingsley's correspondence, The Record Office, Stratford-upon-Avon.
12. Edmund Yates *Recollections and Experiences*, 1884, v. 2, p. 72.
13. George Flower *History of the English Settlement in Edwards County Illinois. Founded in 1817 and 1818 by Morris Birkbeck and George Flower,* Chicago Historical Collection, 1882, passim. see: Richard Foulkes "Edward Flower and The Shakespeare Tercentenary" in *Warwickshire History* vol. v. no. 3. pp. 73–93.
14. Hurford Janes *Flower Breweries*, unpublished typescript in the Stratford-upon-Avon Record Office, pp. 59 and 64.
15. *The Illustrated London News* 7.6.1864.
16. Sarah Flower *Great Aunt Sarah's Diary*, privately published, 1964, p. 51.
17. Hunter op. cit. p. 96.
18. ibid, p. 97.
19. ibid, p. 98.
20. *The Era*, 14.6.1863.
21. *The Era*, 28.6.1863.
22. J W Cole *The Life and Theatrical Times of Charles Kean*, 1858, v. 1. p. 222. For an account of the Keans' Tercentenary Reception in Australia see J M D Hardwick *Emigrant in Motley*, 1954.
23. Letter 9.6.1863 in the J O Halliwell Collection, University of Edinburgh Library.
24. Clement Scott *The Drama of Yesterday and Today*, 1899, v. 1, p. 311.
25. Margaret Webster *The Same Only Different*, 1969, p. 82.
26. *The Times* 2.6.1860.
27. John Cordy Jeaffreson *A Book of Recollections*, 1894, v. 1., p. 164.
28. Henry Vizetelly *Glances Back Through Seventy Years*, 1893, v. 2. p. 105.
29. *The Athenaeum* 25.7.1863.

PLANS AND PROBLEMS

1. James Cox jnr. *The Tercentenary A Retrospect*, 1865, p. 8.
2. Letter 25.8.1863 in the Shakespeare Centre Library.
3. Sarah Flower *Great Aunt Sarah's Diary* privately published 1964, p. 54.
4. W Gordon *The Ethics of the Shakespeare Celebration: A Letter Addressed to a Lady in Sheffield*, 1864, p. 14.
5. John Cordy Jeaffreson *A Book of Recollections*, 1894, v. 1., p. 108.
6. Edmund Yates *Recollections and Experiences*, 1884, v. 2., p. 68. See also Philip Collins "The Rev. John Chippendale Montesquieu Bellew" in *The Listener* 25.11.1971. His son was Kyrle Bellew, the actor.
7. Yates op. cit. v. 2. p. 66.
8. J C M Bellew *Shakespeare's House at New Place*, 1863, pp. 337–8.
9. ibid.
10. Shirley Allen *Samuel Phelps and Sadler's Wells Theatre*, Connecticut 1971, pp. 314–5.
11. John Coleman *Memoirs of Samuel Phelps*, 1886, pp. 241–2.
12. ibid.
13. Letter in the Shakespeare Centre Library Stratford-upon-Avon. An earlier letter of 12.11.1863 inviting Phelps "to subscribe your name to the list of Vice-Presidents" and expressing the hope "that in the Festival Week we may be favoured with your presence and valuable co-operation (should your professional engagements permit of it)" is in the Folger Library, Washington.
14. Letter 12.12.1863 in the Shakespeare Centre Library.
15. Letter 12.12.1863 in the Shakespeare Centre Library.
16. Letter 28.12.1863 in the Shakespeare Centre Library.
17. Letter 16.1.1864 in the Shakespeare Centre Library.
18. Letter 20.1.1864 in the Shakespeare Centre Library.
19. Letter 20.1.1864 in the Shakespeare Centre Library.
20. Letter 21.1.1864 in the Shakespeare Centre Library.
21. Letter in the Shakespeare Centre Library.
22. Robert Hunter *Shakespeare and Stratford-upon-Avon*, 1864, p. 134.
23. Letter from Barnett reproduced in *Morning Star*, as was the whole of the correspondence, 23.3.1864, and in Hunter op. cit. p. 150
24. op. cit. p. 55.
25. Letter – unpublished – 30.3.1864 in the Shakespeare Centre Library.
26. *Tallis's Illustrated Life of London* 23.4.1864.
27. Letter 18.4.1864 from Stella Colas to Dr Kingsley in the Record Office, Stratford-upon-Avon.
28. Letter 7.2.1864 in the Shakespeare Centre Library.
29. Letter 29.3.1864 in the Shakespeare Centre Library.
30. Letter 29.3.1864 in the Shakespeare Centre Library.
31. Letter – to Charles Flower – dated 7.5.1864 in the Shakespeare Centre Library.
32. *The Athenaeum* 25.4.1863. Anne, Lady Ritchie as she became, was most diligent in publishing her father's papers and fiction, writing biographical introductions to the 1898 (13 volumes) and 1911 (26 volumes) editions. Her own literary career never achieved distinction. See Winifred Gérin *Anne Thackeray Ritchie*. London, 1981.
33. Jeaffreson op. cit. v. 1. p. 309.
34. ibid. p. 317.
35. ibid. p. 317.
36. *Illustrated Times* 12.12.1863.
37. op. cit. v. 1. p. 318.

38. op. cit. v. 1. p. 309.
39. *The Daily Telegraph* 6.1.1864.
40. *Illustrated Times* 9.1.1864.
41. *The Times* 20.1.1864.
42. Poem in the Flower scrapbook, v. 1. p. 27 in the Shakespeare Centre Library.
43. *The Athenaeum.*
44. *The Era* 6.3.1864.
45. *The Era* 17.4.1864.

THE PAVILION

1. Address from the Building Sub-Committee 7.9.1863 in the Record Office, Stratford-upon-Avon.
2. J C Trewin *The Night has been Unruly*, 1957, p. 160.
3. *The Era* 24.4.1864.
4. Letter from Telbin 28.4.1864 in the Shakespeare Centre Library, Stratford-upon-Avon.
5. *The Times* 25.4.1864.
6. *The Saturday Review* 30.4.1864.
7. *The Reader* 9.4.1864.
8. Robert Hunter *Shakespeare and Stratford-upon-Avon. Together with A Full Record of the Tercentenary Celebration* 1864, p. 162.
9. The Pavilion contracts, the correspondence about the disputed cost and the final agreement are in the Record Office, Stratford-upon-Avon.
10. The Statement of Account produced for the meeting of 24.8.1864 costed the Pavilion at Branson and Murray's full bill based on a surcharge of £2,052 19s. 11d. which was reduced to £1763 10s. 7d. thereby reducing the grand total by £289 7s. 4d.
11. *All the Year Round* 25.5.1864.
12. A copy of the sale catalogue in the Shakespeare Centre Library.

THE STRATFORD FESTIVAL

1. Robert Hunter *Shakespeare and Stratford*, 1864, p. 168.
2. ibid, p. 172
3. ibid, p. 179.
4. *The Saturday Review* 3.5.1864.
5. Hunter op. cit, p. 191.
6. *All the Year Round* 21.5.1864.
7. Sarah Flower *Great Aunt Sarah's Diary*, 1964, p. 56.
8. op. cit.
9. *The Morning Post* 25.4.1864.
10. *The Times* 23.4.1864.
11. op. cit.
12. Letter 11.4.1864 in the Shakespeare Centre Library. Reproduced in the press including *The Era* 17.4.1864.
13. op. cit. p. 218.
14. *The Daily Telegraph* 26.4.1864.
15. *The Morning Star* 26.4.1864.
16. *The Morning Post* 26.4.1864.
17. Letter 3.5.1864 in the Shakespeare Centre Library.

18. op. cit.
19. op. cit.
20. *The Standard* 29.4.1864.
21. Unacknowledged newspaper cutting in the Flower scrapbook, Shakespeare Centre Library.
22. *The Daily Telegraph* 30.4.1864.
23. Festival programme in the Shakespeare Centre Library.
24. op. cit. p. 37.
25. *The Era* 8.5:1864.
26. op. cit. p. 148.
27. *The Daily Telegraph* 28.4.1864.
28. In the Shakespeare Centre Library.
29. Hunter op. cit. p. 235.
30. *The Era* 8.5.1864.
31. J C Young *A Memoir of Charles Mayne Young Tragedian With Extracts from His Son's Journal*, 1871, v. 2, pp. 292–3.
32. *The Era* 8.5.1864.

THE LONDON PROGRAMME

1. *The Morning Star* 2.5.1864.
2. *Tallis's Illustrated Life of London* 30.4.1864.
3. Henry Morley *The Journal of a London Playgoer*, 1891, p. 275.
4. *Tallis's Illustrated Life of London*, 30.4.1864.
5. op. cit. p. 277.
6. ibid.
7. James Anderson *An Actor's Life*, Newcastle 1902, p. 272.
8. *Tallis's Illustrated Life of London*, 30.4.1864.
9. ibid.
10. op. cit. p. 272.
11. *The Era* 1.5.1864.
12. *The Era* 24.4.1864.
13. *The Era* 24.4.1864. Titiens had not been announced in the programme, another indication of the uncertain organisation.
14. *The Era* 24.4.1864.
15. National Shakespeare Committee programme – copy in British Library.
16. Circular report in the Shakespeare Centre Library.
17. Denis Mack Smith *Garibaldi*, 1957, p. 141.
18. *The Times* 25 April 1864. see Richard Foulkes, "Shakespeare and Garibaldi on Primrose Hill" in *Camden History Review* no. 9, pp. 13–16. An indication of the association between Shakespeare and Garibaldi in the popular imagination is the matching pair of Staffordshire figures produced at the time (P D Gordon Pugh, *Staffordshire Portrait Figures and Allied Subjects of the Victorian Era* 1970, C301 Plate 96. Fig. 281 and Fig. 4). Eliza Cook was one of the few contemporary authors commemorated in a Staffordshire figure.
19. *The Era* 24.4.1864.
20. *The Morning Advertiser* 25.4.1864.
21. ibid.
22. *The Times* 25.4.1864.
23. ibid.
24. ibid.
25. ibid.

26. *The Morning Post* 26.4.1864.
27. *All the Year Round* 21.5.1864.
28. *The Morning Post* 25.4.1864.
29. *The Era* 24.4.1864.

THE LEGACY

1. Copy of the circular in the Flower scrapbook in the Shakespeare Centre Library, Stratford-upon-Avon. The letter was widely published in the press. The fact that the balance is less than the income minus the expenditure is explained by the number of unpaid donations.
2. K J Fielding edt. *The Speeches of Charles Dickens*, 1960, pp. 333–7.
3. Address by Richard Moore, Chairman, and John Bainbridge, Hon. Sec. issued 7.6.1864, copy in the Shakespeare Centre Library.
4. Letter 6.9.1864, in the Folger Library, Washington.
5. *The Era* 31.7.1864.
6. Le Chevalier de Chatelain, *Notre Monument par Le Chevalier de Chatelain. Documents Dédies aux futurs vivants de 23 Avril 1964, par servir à la lamentable histoire de feu le Shakespeare National Committee du 23 Avril 1864; et un peu aussi à l'histoire de l'auteur*, 1867, p. 126.
7. *The Era* 23.7.1871.
8. ibid.
9. *The Era* 2.3.1873.
10. *The Era* 9.3.1873. Copy of "The Shakespeare Oak on Primrose Hill. Appeal on Shakespeare's Day" in the Shakespeare Library, Birmingham City Reference Library.
11. *The Era* 4.5.1873.
12. *The Era* 18.4.1875.
13. J Cordy Jeaffreson *A Book of Recollections*, 1894, v. 1, p. 316.
14. Letter 7.10.1982 from Miss M V Stokes, Coutts' Archivist.
15. On 23 April 1964 the ceremony was performed by Dame Edith Evans, who spoke lines specially composed by V C Clinton-Baddeley. A retrospective look at the Tercentenary was made by Stanley Wells and T J B Spencer in "Shakespeare in Celebration" in T J B Spencer (ed.): *Shakespeare: A Celebration*, 1964, pp. 121–7.
16. A Poet's Fountain by Thomas Thornycroft was erected at the junction between Park Lane and Hamilton Place in 1875; it was demolished in 1949. See: Lord Edward Gleichen *London's Open Air Statuary*, 1928, p. 163.
17. See Geoffrey Whitworth *The Making of a National Theatre*, 1951, and John Elsom and Nicholas Tomalin *The History of the National Theatre*, 1978.
18. Report in the Flower Scrapbook in the Shakespeare Centre Library.
19. *The Builder*, 7.10.1865, together with a copy of Gibbs's design.
20. Laurence Irving *Henry Irving*, 1951, p. 487.
21. Letter in the Flower Scrapbook in the Shakespeare Centre Library.
22. Robert Hunter *Shakespeare and Stratford-upon-Avon*, 1864, p. 241.
23. *The Athenaeum* 9.7.1864.
24. *The Saturday Review* 1.9.1864.
25. J Cox jnr. *The Tercentenary. A Retrospect*, 1865, p. 6.
26. *The Daily Telegraph* 21.3.1877.
27. Ruth Ellis *The Shakespeare Memorial Theatre*, 1948, p. 9. See also Sally Beauman *The Royal Shakespeare Company: A History of Ten Decades*, 1982.
28. *The Times* 23.4.1864.

Selected Bibliography

All the Year Round

Shirley Allen *Samuel Phelps and Sadler's Wells Theatre*, Connecticut, 1971

James Anderson *An Actor's Life*, Newcastle, 1902

The Athenaeum

Michael Baker *The Rise of the Victorian Actor*, London, 1978

Sally Beauman *The Royal Shakespeare Company: A History of Ten Decades*, Oxford/London, 1982

J C M Bellew *Shakespeare's House at New Place*, London 1863

Ivor Brown and George Fearon *Amazing Monument A Short History of the Shakespeare Industry*, London, 1939

The Builder

Mrs. Charles Calvert *Sixty-Eight Years on the Stage*, London, 1911

Le Chevalier de Chatelain *Notre Monument par Le Chevalier de Chatelain. Documents Dédies aux futurs vivants de 23 Avril 1964, par servir à la lamentable histoire de feu le Shakespeare National Committee du 23 Avril 1864; et un peu, aussi à l'histoire de l'auteur*, London, 1867

J W Cole *The Life and Theatrical Times of Charles Kean*, London, 1858

J Coleman *Memoirs of Samuel Phelps*, London, 1886

J Payne Collier *Memoirs of Edward Alleyn, founder of Dulwich College*, London, 1841

J Payne Collier *The Alleyn Papers*, London, 1843

J Cox jnr. *The Tercentenary A Retrospect*, Stratford, 1865

William Creswick *An Autobiography*, London, 1889

Alan Crosby *A History of Woking*, Chichester, 1982

The Daily Telegraph

Christine Deelman *The Great Shakespeare Jubilee*, London, 1964

Charles Dickens *Our Mutual Friend*, London, 1864

The Dickensian

W Hepworth Dixon *Weekly Gossip*, London, 1866

Henry Dodd *The Royal Dramatic College Correspondence Concerning Proposed Gift of Land by Mr. Henry Dodd*, London, 1859

Ruth Ellis *The Shakespeare Memorial Theatre*, London, 1948

John Elsom and Nicholas Tomalin *The History of the National Theatre*, London, 1978

The Era

Helena Faucit, Lady Martin, *On Some of Shakespeare's Female Characters*, Edinburgh and London, 1887

K J Fielding (edt) *The Speeches of Charles Dickens*, Oxford/London, 1960

Edward Flower *Tercentenary Scrapbooks*, Shakespeare Birthplace Trust Library, Stratford-upon-Avon

George Flower *History of the English Settlement in Edwards County Illinois. Founded in 1817 and 1818 by Morris Birkbeck and George Flower*, Chicago, 1882

Sarah Flower *Great Aunt Sarah's Diary*, Stratford (privately printed), 1964

John Forster *The Life of Charles Dickens*, London, 1874

Dewey Ganzel *Fortune and Men's Eyes. The career of John Payne Collier*, Oxford, 1982.

Winifred Gérin *Anne Thackeray Ritchie*, London, 1981

Lord Edward Gleichen *London's Open Air Statuary*, London, 1928

W Gordon *The Ethics of the Shakespeare Celebration: A Letter Addressed to a Lady in Sheffield*, London, 1864

A History of the Shakespeare Memorial Stratford-upon-Avon. Published for the Council of the Shakespeare Memorial Association, London, 1879

J O Halliwell-Phillips *Life of Shakespeare*, London, 1848

J O Halliwell-Phillips *An Historical Account of New Place*, London, 1864

J M D Hardwick *Emigrant in Motley*, London, 1954

Susanne Howe *Geraldine Jewsbury Her Life and Errors*, London, 1935

Robert Hunter *Shakespeare and Stratford-Upon-Avon Together With a Full Report of the Tercentenary Celebration*, London, 1864

The Illustrated London News

Illustrated Times

Laurence Irving *Henry Irving*, London, 1951

Hurford Jane *Flower Breweries*, unpublished

J Cordy Jeaffreson *A Book of Recollections*, London, 1894

T C Kemp and J C Trewin *The Stratford Festival*, Birmingham, 1953

Joseph Macleod *The Actor's Right to Act*, London, 1981

Mrs. A Mathews *Memoirs of Charles Mathews Comedian*, London, 1838

Theodore Martin *Helena Faucit (Lady Martin)*, Edinburgh & London, 1900

Henry Morley *The Journal of a London Playgoer*, London, 1891

The Morning Advertiser

The Morning Post

The Morning Star

The National Shakespeare Committee and The Late Mr. Thackeray Signed The Lounger in the Clubs, London, 1864

Nineteenth Century Theatre Research

Carola Oman *David Garrick*, London, 1958

W May Phelps and John Forbes-Robertson *The Life and Life-Work of Samuel Phelps*, London, 1886

Una Pope-Hennessy *Charles Dickens*, London, 1945

P D Gordon Pugh *Staffordshire Portrait Figures and Allied Subjects of The Victorian Period*, London, 1970

Gordon N Ray *The Letters and Private Papers of W M Thackeray*, London, 1946

George Rowell *Queen Victoria Goes to the Theatre*, London, 1978

George Rowell (edt) *Victorian Dramatic Criticism*, London, 1971

The Saturday Review

George Scharf jnr. *A Few Observations Connected with the Chandos Portrait of Shakespeare Presented to the National Portrait Gallery by the Earl of Ellesmere 1856*, London, 1864

S Schoenbaum *Shakespeare, the Globe and the World*, London, 1979

Clement Scott *The Drama of Yesterday and Today*, London, 1899

Clement Scott and Cecil Howard *Edward Leman Blanchard*, London, 1891

D Mack Smith *Garibaldi*, London, 1957

Charles Roach Smith *Retrospections Social and Archaeological*, London, 1886

T J B Spencer (edt) *Shakespeare: A Celebration*, London, 1964

Aron Y Stavisky *Shakespeare and the Victorians*, Oklahoma, 1969

Johanne M Stockholm *Garrick's Folly*, London, 1964

The Standard

Tallis's Illustrated Life of London

The Tercentenary or the Three Hundredth Birthday of William Shakespeare by Messrs. E Moses and Son, London, 1864

Theatre Notebook

The Times

J C Trewin *The Night has been Unruly*, London, 1957

J C Trewin *The Pomping Folk*, London, 1968

Henry Vizetelly *Glances Back Through Seventy Years*, London, 1892

Lou Warwick *Theatre Unroyal*, Northampton, 1974

Margaret Webster *The Same Only Different*, London, 1969

J R and S E Whiteman *Victorian Woking*, Woking, 1970

Geoffrey Whitworth *The Making of a National Theatre*, London, 1951

Edmund Yates *Recollections and Experiences*, London, 1884

Edmund Yates *Mr. Thackeray, Mr. Yates and The Garrick Club. The Correspondence and Facts. Stated by Edmund Yates*, London, 1858

J C Young *A Memoir of Charles Mayne Young Tragedian With Extracts from His Son's Journal*, London, 1871

Index